S. Hrg. 113–632

LEADING THE WAY: ADAPTING TO SOUTH FLORIDA'S CHANGING COASTLINE

FIELD HEARING

BEFORE THE

SUBCOMMITTEE ON SCIENCE AND SPACE

OF THE

COMMITTEE ON COMMERCE, SCIENCE, AND TRANSPORTATION UNITED STATES SENATE

ONE HUNDRED THIRTEENTH CONGRESS

SECOND SESSION

APRIL 22, 2014

Printed for the use of the Committee on Commerce, Science, and Transportation

U.S. GOVERNMENT PUBLISHING OFFICE

94–339 PDF   WASHINGTON : 2015

(II)

CONTENTS

LEADING THE WAY: ADAPTING TO SOUTH FLORIDA'S CHANGING COASTLINE

TUESDAY, APRIL 22, 2014

U.S. SENATE,
SUBCOMMITTEE ON SCIENCE AND SPACE,
COMMITTEE ON COMMERCE, SCIENCE, AND TRANSPORTATION,
Miami Beach, FL.

The Subcommittee met, pursuant to notice, at 10 a.m. at the Miami Beach City Hall, Commission Chambers, 1700 Convention Center Drive, Miami Beach, Florida, Hon. Bill Nelson, presiding.

OPENING STATEMENT OF HON. BILL NELSON, U.S. SENATOR FROM FLORIDA

Senator NELSON. The meeting of the Senate Commerce Committee will come to order. And I want to thank all of you for coming. We have a capacity crowd here today.

It is a topic of considerable concern to a great number of people, but it is a topic of concern that a lot of people have not even considered, and that is climate change and the direct effects, on those of us that live on the coast because of sea level rise. And so we have titled this hearing today—this field hearing of the Senate Commerce, Science, and Transportation Committee—we have titled it, "Leading the Way: Adapting to South Florida's Changing Coastline."

Now, before I make my opening remarks, I wanted to extend the courtesy to the Members of Congress in the South Florida delegation who wanted to come by and participate with us today. They will not be a part of the formal panel. And so I want Congressman Garcia to share a couple of comments with us.

Congressman?

STATEMENT OF HON. JOE GARCIA, U.S. REPRESENTATIVE FROM FLORIDA

Mr. GARCIA. Thank you, Senator.

First off, I just wanted to thank you for doing this. Obviously, I represent probably ground zero, if there is one, when it comes to global warming. I represent the Florida Keys and South Florida. And there is not a week that goes by that this issue doesn't come before us in one way or another.

Last week alone, we had a hearing where we met with agricultural leaders in South Dade, one of the most productive areas for agriculture in the country, and they are having water intrusion problems that they have never suffered before. We met, the week before that, with leaders of the Everglades and the Everglades community and discussed the issues they are dealing with.

And, of course, I am also the southernmost Congressman of the United States, so I represent the Florida Keys and the issues that they already feel.

So, as part of that, sort of coming off of your leadership with this, we are doing a series of events on Earth Week. This Thursday at 3:30 at the University of Miami, we will be having a similar discussion with business, the effects of sea level rise and the impacts it will have in South Florida.

Even dogs are concerned on this issue.

[Laughter.]

Mr. GARCIA. So we always appreciate that.

Just very quickly, I just want to recognize some folks that have given tremendous leadership on this. And one in particular is our mutual friend, Harvey Ruvin, who has been a leader on this for decades, before this was a popular thing.

[Applause.]

Mr. GARCIA. He was talking about this when I didn't know what it meant. And so it is an important thing, and I want to recognize that.

And, finally——

Senator NELSON. He was talking about this when you were an infant.

[Laughter.]

Mr. GARCIA. Thank you, Senator. Thank you.

Mr. RUVIN. Now, wait a second——

[Laughter.]

Mr. GARCIA. I agree with that statement.

[Laughter.]

Mr. GARCIA. But this is important to all of us, and how it affects us.

And, finally, it is about being pragmatic, Senator. You have shown the ability in the Senate to be pragmatic, to find common sense solutions to the issues before us. If we posture this as an ideological debate, we don't deal with the problem.

And while this may be a problem, it could be a tremendous opportunity for South Florida, for the entire country, because on the issues of technology that can affect these things, on the issues of finding alternative energy, on so many issues, Florida and the United States is a leader. I know you have been part of that leadership group.

And I thank the Mayor for hosting us, as well as the City of Miami Beach, where I am a part-time resident.

Thank you very much, Senator, for doing this.

Senator NELSON. Thank you, Congressman.

[Applause.]

Senator NELSON. Other than the panel that will testify today— of course Harvey has already been acknowledged—Mayor Cindy Lerner of Pinecrest is here.

[Applause.]

Senator NELSON. And we have several members of the City Commission of Miami Beach. Would you stand and be recognized?

[Applause.]

Senator NELSON. I want to thank all of you for coming today. We especially thank the City Commission and the mayor for hosting us here.

And I specifically wanted to come here because this is ground zero. High tide, there is flooding. Over the last 50 years—we will hear testimony—sea level rise has been in Florida any place from five to eight inches. It is real. And yet some of our colleagues in the Senate deny it. Jim Inhofe, a good person, a good Senator for his State of Oklahoma, he debunks the idea. But he is one of a very few.

What happens in the discussion of climate change is the fact that the media, wanting to be fair and balanced, present it as if it is 50–50. But look at the scientific community and the proof that we hope to hear today to enter into the *Congressional Record.*

Now, this is an official meeting of the U.S. Senate. And testimony is being recorded by our recorder, Senate recorder, and it will be a part of the official record of the U.S. Senate and the Committee on Commerce.

Now, we particularly—it is just coincidental, this is the 44th anniversary of Earth Day. And so here in South Florida, ground zero, to discuss with Floridians what we are doing to protect our coastal ecosystems and economies despite rising sea levels.

So you say, well, why don't we put up dikes like Holland? But Holland has a completely different terra firma. We are on this massive substrate of limestone and coquina rock, which is porous and it is infused by water. And so you could put up a dike, but it is not going to do any good, because through the substrate, which is like Swiss cheese, the water flows.

And so we have to come up with innovative, new kinds of solutions for what in fact is happening, despite what one-tenth of one percent of the folks that talk about this issue of climate change say. We ought to be listening to the 99 percent of scientific evidence.

I am also glad to return to my native parts. I was born in Miami. As a matter of fact, I was born in the Victoria hospital. It is no longer a hospital. At one point, it was a psychiatric hospital.

[Laughter.]

Senator NELSON. It was, and I guess today is, a mixed-use medical facility over near the old Orange Bowl.

Miami was a totally different community back then. As a matter of fact, I will never forget, as a kid, at age six, I was in the Orange Bowl parade. Now, that was held on New Year's Eve, and that was one of the big social events of Miami. And it would start along Biscayne, and it would go down to Flagler and then turn west on Flagler. At age six in the Orange Bowl parade, you know what I was? I was a Latin dancer.

[Laughter.]

Senator NELSON. I was raised on Biscayne Bay the first years of my life. And I want to ensure that South Florida continues to thrive as this wonderful fabric of mix that has become the center, a microcosm of the Western Hemisphere. I want to see us continue to thrive economically and as a vacation destination, a beautiful place to live and do business.

So we best get about the process of recognizing what is happening all around us. Now, we are going to have to face it head-on, which is the purpose of the hearing. The Federal Government certainly needs to step up and do its part. We need to lead the way and cut down on pollution from cars and power plants, and I will go on and on.

Now, since the Congresswoman has arrived, Congresswoman, I want to give you a moment. I am going to stop my opening comments for brief comments from you.

STATEMENT OF HON. FREDERICA WILSON, U.S. REPRESENTATIVE FROM FLORIDA

Ms. WILSON. Good morning. I am fighting a frog in my throat. But it is pleasure to be here this morning. And our great Senator, thank you so much for organizing this event.

And this is a very, very scary subject for South Florida. And we have read so many op-eds about what we can foresee in the future, and I even wrote one for the *Sun Sentinel* back in December. There was one in *Rolling Stone* and the *Miami Herald* that just frightened everyone.

So we are hoping that people in Congress and in our State legislatures will begin to take climate change seriously. It is something that we cannot afford to ignore. People say it is going to cost so much money. Well, whatever it costs, we should begin to spend that money.

And I am very pleased that so many of our counties throughout the state of Florida have begun their own initiatives, being very creative to address this issue. Because before we know it and not so very long from now, we will be losing so much of our coast.

So thank you so much for bringing this important issue to our community. I serve on the Science, Space, and Technology Committee and as the Ranking Member of Technology in the Florida House of Representatives. And it is a pleasure to be here and to listen to all of the testimony, because every time we listen, we learn. And every time someone talks about it, the conversation becomes larger and larger, and maybe some of the people who don't even believe in science—some of them serve on the Committee with me. They don't believe in science, period.

[Laughter.]

Ms. WILSON. They will begin to listen and will begin to get on board with this train that we have to set up.

Thank you so much.

Senator NELSON. Thank you, Congresswoman.

[Applause.]

Senator NELSON. May I ask the witnesses to come up, please?

As they are getting settled, as we get into this topic, we want to make sure that our resources, not just funding for research, not just funding for infrastructure, but research and brain power, is focused on cutting-edge science and the technology that will develop from it and that will help us adapt and respond to the effects of sea level rise.

So what we have in this room today are the leaders who are concerned about this issue. Now, by the way, we invited the rest of the members of the Commerce Committee. My colleague, Senator Rubio, on the Committee is out of town.

But my colleague, Senator Sheldon Whitehouse of Rhode Island, because of the Easter recess, he is actually coming to Florida this Thursday and Friday and will be doing a series of climate change events, first starting on Thursday, where I will join him in Jacksonville, and then he will progress on further south. And it is going to end up, I think, in Broward on Friday.

So, all of you leaders, you aren't waiting on anyone to start preparing for climate change. We can't afford to, with Florida being ground zero. For example, according to the National Climate Assessment, about half of $1 trillion in coastal property valuation would be at risk given two feet of sea level rise in this state. Now, if the last 50 years has had five to eight inches, you can see that is right down the line.

So to reduce the costly and damaging impacts of sea level rise, we are going to hear about how some of our towns and cities have been making upgrades to stormwater and wastewater treatment systems.

And, oh, by the way, the reason, when the rains come, that you don't flood is because we have a flood control system, which, by the way, we are trying to completely replumb as we restore the Everglades. It was a mistake that was done over the course of the past century of draining the Everglades.

But for the urban areas, drainage is based on gravity. And it is not the movie.

[Laughter.]

Senator NELSON. Well, if the sea level rises, what happens to that ability when the rains come and the floods occur and you need to get the water off of the neighborhoods by gravity? You can't do it. So you have to go to much more expensive systems of pumping.

And that is just one of the little things that communities in South Florida and the Everglades restoration projects are all having to face.

And so today we are going to hear from a very distinguished panel. First, we are going to hear from the Mayor of Miami Beach, Mayor Philip Levine. And he is going to discuss the key actions his administration has proposed to keep the tidal floods out of Miami Beach.

Get ready. The high tides are coming in October. So we are going to have a real demonstration here of something that is real.

And then we are going to hear from Dr. Piers Sellers, former NASA astronaut, currently the Deputy Director for Sciences and Exploration at Goddard Space Flight Center in suburban Maryland. And he will help us understand the facts of climate change and sea level rise.

Dr. Sellers, what flight did you fly on?

Mr. SELLERS. 112, 121, 132, sir.

Senator NELSON. Three flights. This is the real deal right here.

[Applause.]

Senator NELSON. And the last one was?

Mr. SELLERS. 132, which was 2010. We were up there and saw the Gulf oil spill.

Senator NELSON. He was 2010. The space shuttle program was shut down, of necessity, in 2011. Two more flights after Dr. Sellers. We had 135 flights, and, as you remember, two of those were lost and 14 souls lost.

And so, thanks to the great work of organizations like NASA, there can be no denying that climate is changing and that we are seeing the effects right now. And we are going to hear about some of NASA's satellites that are so important for us to calibrate and measure.

And then we are going to hear from Broward County Commissioner Kristin Jacobs on how the Southeast Florida Regional Climate Change Compact uses Federal resources and data for adaptation strategies for the impacts of climate change.

And then we will hear from Dr. Fred Bloetscher, who is an Associate Professor at Florida Atlantic. He will cover climate change aspects and impacts to Florida's infrastructure as well as to its coastal and wetland ecosystems.

And then we are going to hear from Bill Talbert, Miami-Dade Tourism and Convention Bureau, so that we can fully understand the economic importance of the coastlines. Florida's coast is home to 75 percent of our population.

Our population, by the way, in Florida, if you didn't know it, is a big deal. This year, we are overtaking New York in population. By the end of the year, we will be the third largest state, close to 20 million people. Seventy-five percent of that population lives on the coast. And, of course, in our economy, especially here in South Florida, tourism is a key contributing factor.

And, finally, I have asked a representative of the reinsurance industry to talk about how private sector uses of climate change data will help them in their risk modeling.

Now, you may recall that before I came to this job I had the toughest job that I have ever had in public service, and that was Florida's elected insurance commissioner. And during that time in the 1990s, I could not get insurance companies to pay attention—American insurance companies to pay attention—to climate change and sea level rise. In the 1990s, European insurance companies were beginning to pay attention, but not American.

And so Dr. Megan Linkin, she is the natural hazards expert from Swiss Re, to explain how their industry has no choice but to try to quantify the cost of climate change impacts to measure what is the risk and how much they ought to charge for it.

So I thank everybody that is here. We have a very heavy subject.

Now, what we are going to do, we are going to take your written statements, we are going to insert them into the permanent record of the Committee, and I am going to ask you all if you would share with us, about five minutes each, your comments, and then we will get into questions. I may be questioning you as you go, but we will see how it progresses.

So, Mr. Mayor, we will call on you first.

STATEMENT OF HON. PHILIP LEVINE, MAYOR, CITY OF MIAMI BEACH, FLORIDA

Mr. LEVINE. Thank you. And, Senator, first of all, my apologies from that barking constituent that you heard upstairs. He wanted to come down here and testify, but we wouldn't let him.

I may go longer than 5 minutes, so cut me off at any time.

Senator NELSON. Mr. Mayor, whenever you have a bomb-sniffing dog, that dog is always welcome.

[Laughter.]

Mr. LEVINE. I wish he was that useful.

[Laughter.]

Mr. LEVINE. Subcommittee Chairman Nelson and distinguished members of the Subcommittee, it is an honor to be here today to share with you how the City of Miami Beach is responding and adapting to the impacts of climate change.

I am Philip Levine, Mayor of the City of Miami Beach. For almost 30 years, I have been an integral member of the Miami Beach community. Over the years, I have established a number of successful beach-based businesses, creating hundreds of job opportunities for local and area residents while contributing to the city's tax-revenue base.

In 2010, I was tapped by President Obama's Secretary of Commerce to serve on a Task Force advising on U.S. tourism. Through my involvement with the task force, I worked to strengthen the nation's growing international tourism industry, which in turn strengthened our economy.

Now, as the Mayor of Miami Beach, I face the challenge to mitigate the tidal flooding our city is currently experiencing as a result of rising seas and to address other pressing issues associated with climate change.

Before I begin, I would like to welcome you and introduce you to our unique city. Miami Beach is a barrier island located in southeast Florida between Biscayne Bay and the Atlantic Ocean that was developed by filling in natural mangrove wetlands with dredge soil over a porous limestone base.

Our urbanized island is situated within the sensitive habitat of the Biscayne Bay Aquatic Preserve and has flourished because of its natural assets, including parks, natural and man-made waterways, sea grass beds, mangrove shorelines, sand dunes, and over 7 miles of white sandy beaches.

Miami Beach is globally recognized for our rich history as a cultural and entertainment tourism capital and our role as an international center for innovation and business. In 2012, the city drew 5.8 million overnight visitors, which spent $9.2 billion or 42 percent of the tourism revenue generated in Miami-Dade County.

Miami Beach's real estate, including an inventory of 1,516 properties that contribute to the National Register of Historic Places and 12 historic districts, is worth over $23 billion. Despite being only 0.3 percent of Miami-Dade County's land mass, this value represents 12 percent of the County's total real estate value.

Florida and the U.S. cannot afford to lose our city. However, due to climate change, the future of Miami Beach and other coastal communities has become more uncertain.

In the last century, scientists have encountered indelible evidence that our climate is warming. The Intergovernmental Panel on Climate Change has reported that over the period of 1901 to 2010 the global mean sea level rose by 0.19 meters, which is over half a foot. In 2012, a U.S. Geological Survey study concluded that sea levels along the East Coast of the country will rise three to four times faster than the global average over the next century. And the U.S. Army Corps of Engineers has projected that the water around Miami could rise up to 0.6 meters, which is two feet, by 2060.

These projections are alarming, particularly for a city like Miami Beach that has an average elevation of 4.4 feet using the North American Vertical Datum of 1988. Our geographic location and low-lying topography make us inherently vulnerable to flooding, storm surge, and other climate change impacts. Therefore, it is imperative that our city is prepared to face these growing challenges so we can continue to thrive and contribute to the success of the region and our Nation.

Sea level rise is our reality in Miami Beach. We are past the point of debating the existence of climate change and are now focusing on adapting to current and future threats. My testimony here today is to share with you the anticipated short-term and long-term challenges Miami Beach is facing due to climate change, to highlight the mitigation and adaptation strategies we currently have in place to make our city resilient in a changing climate, and to instill a sense of urgency in the Federal Government to prioritize climate change action and policy.

Climate Change Challenges: Miami Beach's most pressing climate change challenge is sea level rise, because we are already seeing its effects firsthand. In recent years, Miami Beach has observed an increased frequency of urban flooding caused by higher tides, elevated groundwater levels, and oversaturated soils.

Street flooding so regularly impacts our city that residents have become familiar with its effects on city operations and their daily lives. It is not uncommon to worry about vehicles parked in areas with quickly rising tidal waters or to observe residents wading barefoot through knee-high flood waters to access their homes and local businesses.

This reality is not acceptable, and it is getting worse. During last years king tides in October, there was 1½ feet of saltwater that inundated the streets. According to the National Oceanic and Atmospheric Administration, the king tides this October are anticipated to be three feet and nine inches above mean high water, which is almost three inches higher than our city saw last year.

Miami Beach also recognizes storm surge as a pressing climate challenge. Like sea level rise, storm surge raises the waters surrounding Miami Beach above average levels, resulting in flooding, and causes damages to upland properties and infrastructure. During Hurricane Sandy in 2012, we experienced waves as high as 10 feet, which caused significant flooding and beach erosion throughout our city.

While Miami Beach is familiar with hurricanes, scientific studies indicate that extreme weather events, such as storms, floods, and hurricanes, will increase in frequency and intensity.

Since I entered office in November 2013, I have made it my top priority to mitigate flooding and other climate change impacts. In 2014, I formed a Blue Ribbon Panel on Flooding Mitigation to oversee the city's response to flooding and provide a comprehensive and visionary approach to flood management and sea level rise adaptation.

The panel's mission extends beyond providing guidance on stormwater design criteria and helping to prioritize infrastructure upgrades. For example, the panel has also made recommendations to increase base flood building elevations and has discussed the effects of climate change on our urban design. The City Commission relies on the panel's recommendations to implement short-term strategies and long-term policies and solutions.

In coordination with the panel, Miami Beach is working diligently to address existing flooding concerns. Guided by our updated Stormwater Management Master Plan, we are upgrading our aging gravity-based stormwater infrastructure with tidal control valves, pump stations, and other innovative structures that will improve drainage by preventing seawater from entering the system and by quickly expelling flood waters from urban areas, even during periods of elevated tidal or water table levels.

Senator NELSON. Mr. Mayor?

Mr. LEVINE. Yes, sir.

Senator NELSON. We are going to wrap up here.

[The prepared statement of Mr. Levine follows:]

PREPARED STATEMENT OF HON. PHILIP LEVINE, MAYOR,
CITY OF MIAMI BEACH, FLORIDA

Subcommittee Chairman Nelson and distinguished members of the Subcommittee, it is an honor to be here today to share with you how the City of Miami Beach is responding and adapting to the impacts of climate change.

I am Philip Levine, Mayor of the City of Miami Beach. For almost 30 years, I have been an integral member of the Miami Beach community. Over the years, I have established a number of successful Miami Beach-based businesses, creating hundreds of job opportunities for local and area residents while contributing to the city's tax-revenue base. In 2010, I was tapped by President Obama's Secretary of Commerce to serve on a Task Force advising on U.S. tourism. Through my involvement with the Task Force, I worked to strengthen the Nation's growing international tourism industry—which in turn strengthened our economy. Now as the Mayor of Miami Beach, I face the challenge to mitigate the tidal flooding our city is currently experiencing as a result of rising seas and to address other pressing issues associated with climate change.

Before I begin, I would like to welcome you and introduce you to our unique city. Miami Beach is a barrier island located in southeast Florida between Biscayne Bay and the Atlantic Ocean that was developed by filling in natural mangrove wetlands with dredge spoil over a porous limestone base. The island is situated within the sensitive habitat of the Biscayne Bay Aquatic Preserve, and is has flourished by linking the urban environment to its natural capital including parks, natural and man-made waterways, sea grass beds, mangrove shorelines, sand dunes, and over seven miles of white, sandy beaches. Miami Beach is globally-recognized for our rich history as a cultural and entertainment tourism capital and our role as an international center for innovation and business.

In 2012, the city drew 5.8 million overnight visitors, which spent $9.2 billion or 42 percent of the tourism revenue generated in Miami-Dade County. Miami Beach's real estate, including an inventory of 1,516 properties that contribute to the National Register of Historic Places and 12 historic districts, is worth over $23 billion. Despite being only 0.3 percent of Miami-Dade County's land mass, this value represents 12 percent of the County's total real estate value. Florida and the U.S. cannot afford to lose our city. However, due to climate change, the future of Miami Beach and other coastal communities has become more uncertain.

In the last century, scientists have encountered indelible evidence that our climate is warming. The Intergovernmental Panel for Climate Change has reported that over the period of 1901 to 2010, the global mean sea level rose by 0.19 meters, which is over half a foot. In 2012, a U.S. Geological Survey study concluded that sea levels along the east coast of the country will rise three to four times faster than the global average over the next century and the U.S. Army Corps of Engineers has projected that the water around Miami could rise up to 24 inches by 2060. These projections are alarming, particularly for a city like Miami Beach that has an average elevation of 4.4 feet North American Vertical Datum 1988.

Our geographic location and low-lying topography make us inherently vulnerable to flooding, storm surge, and other climate change impacts. Therefore, it is imperative that our city is prepared to face these growing challenges so we can continue to thrive and contribute to the success of the region and our Nation. Sea level rise is our reality in Miami Beach. We are past the point of debating the existence of climate change and are now focusing on adapting to current and future threats. My testimony here today is to share with you the anticipated short-term and long-term challenges Miami Beach is facing due to climate change, to highlight the mitigation and adaption strategies we currently have in place to make our city resilient in a changing climate, and to instill a sense of urgency in the Federal Government to prioritize climate change action and policy

Climate Change Challenges

Miami Beach's most pressing climate change challenge is sea level rise because we are already seeing its effects first-hand. In recent years, Miami Beach has observed an increased frequency of urban flooding caused by higher high tides, elevated groundwater levels, and oversaturated soils. Flooding so regularly impacts our city that residents have become familiar with its effect on city operations and their daily lives. It is not uncommon to worry about vehicles parked in areas with quickly rising tidal waters or to observe residents wading barefoot through knee-high flood waters to access their homes and local businesses. This reality is not acceptable and it is getting worse. During last year's king tides in October there was one and a half feet of salt water that inundated the streets. According to the National Oceanic and Atmospheric Administration, the king tides this October are anticipated to be three feet and nine inches above mean high water, which is almost three inches higher than our city saw last year.

Miami Beach also recognizes storm surge as a pressing climate change challenge. Like sea level rise, storm surge raises the waters surrounding Miami Beach above average levels, results in flooding, and causes damage to upland properties and infrastructure. During Hurricane Sandy in 2012, we experienced waves as high as 10 feet, which caused significant flooding and beach erosion throughout our city. While Miami Beach is familiar with hurricanes, scientific studies indicate that extreme weather events such as storms, floods, and hurricanes will increase in frequency and intensity.

Since I entered office in November 2013, I have made it my top priority to mitigate flooding and other climate change impacts. In January 2014, I formed a Blue Ribbon Panel on Flooding Mitigation to oversee the city's response to flooding and provide a comprehensive and visionary approach to flood management and sea level rise adaptation. The Panel's mission extends beyond providing guidance on stormwater design criteria and helping to prioritize infrastructure upgrades. For example, the Panel has also made recommendations to increase base flood elevations and has discussed the effects of climate change on our urban design. The City Commission relies on the Panel's recommendations to implement short-term strategies and long-term policies and solutions.

In coordination with the Panel, Miami Beach is working diligently to address existing flooding concerns. Guided by our updated Stormwater Management Master Plan, we are upgrading our aging gravity-based stormwater infrastructure with tidal control valves, pump stations, and other innovative structures that will improve drainage by preventing seawater from entering the system and by quickly expelling flood waters from urban areas, even during periods of elevated tidal or water table levels. Per the provisions of our stormwater management master plan, the standards used to design these on-going drainage projects will be updated as new data, including sea level rise projections and local ground water hydrology, become available. We are building a long-term sea level rise adaptation plans that focus on flexible low-regret strategies to accommodate a changing environment but that can be developed into more robust plans as existing uncertainty diminishes.

The city is also reinforcing the engineering and natural buffers surrounding our city to protect us against storm surge. We are prioritizing upgrades to the 3 miles of public seawall surrounding our city so they meet stringent design standards that take into account projected sea level rise and storm surge. Additionally, we are working with experts to identify mechanisms, like public-private partnerships, for upgrading the 57 miles of private seawalls. In coastal areas without seawalls, we are looking at natural infrastructure, such as building a more robust beach and dune system and living shorelines, for storm protection. For example, our on-going dune restoration and enhancement project that uses an ecosystem-based approach to restore the health of the dune system so it can continue to provide critical storm surge and erosion protection along our eastern coast.

Miami Beach is also committed to enhancing the environmental sustainability of our city. The Intergovernmental Panel on Climate Change concludes that the continued emission of greenhouse gases will cause further changes in the climate system, such as a warmer ocean, less sea ice, and higher sea levels. Therefore, in accordance with our municipal sustainability plan, the city is also making a concerted effort to reduce our carbon emissions in our city operations through a platform that leads our residents by example. Most recently, the City leveraged Federal Stimulus Funds to complete facility lighting and lighting control upgrades, HVAC control retrofits, water fixture replacements, and a geothermal district cooling plant optimization to reduce energy usage in select city facilities. We are also expanding the city fleet to include more vehicles that produce low-emissions and use alternative fuel options.

Thanks to the support we have received from the State and Federal governments, we are reducing the number of single-occupancy vehicles by developing a more robust multi-modal transportation system and improving the availability of public transit options. We are designing our system using a complete streets approach to improve pedestrian and bicycle connectivity throughout the city and encourage the use of alternative transportation. We are also working to increase the incentives available to residents who are helping us reach our reduced carbon emission goals, such as users of low-emission and electric vehicles.

Moving into the future, Miami Beach is looking to become the nexus of innovation for short-term and long-term climate change planning. We are looking within and beyond our borders for innovative solutions to our climate change challenges. In September 2013, the city hosted a one-day seminar where experts from southeast Florida and the Kingdom of the Netherlands engaged in multidisciplinary, cross-cultural discussions designed to explore if, where, and how Dutch approaches to water management, flood protection, and urban design are relevant in making our city more resilient. Over 100 individuals, including Miami Beach residents and business owners, government agency representatives, scientists, and students, were in attendance. Thanks to these collaborative discussions, we are currently evaluating water management strategies that we had not previously considered like the addition of water retention to public and private properties and of water storage components to new structures.

We will continue to foster and support information exchange by working with our local, national, and international partners like the Southeast Florida Regional Climate Change Compact (the Compact). The Compact is a collaborative effort among Palm Beach, Broward, Miami-Dade and Monroe Counties, their municipalities and partners who have come together to facilitate regional planning efforts. In 2012, the Compact released the Regional Climate Action Plan that provides an integrated framework to guide policies that align regional goals; reduce green house gas emissions; address vulnerabilities, such as water supply; preserve natural resources; effectively respond to risk and emergencies; and incorporates public outreach. Our ongoing participation with the Compact is helping us and its members coordinate resources and develop win-win strategies that accomplish multiple goals to address climate change impacts.

Resiliency Planning

Miami Beach will continue to face numerous challenges in the future and is committed to seeking and implementing solutions to reduce climate change impacts. Over the next five years, we will spend over $300 million to complete neighborhood drainage projects that will alleviate chronic street-level flooding and reduce property flooding concerns. We are also funding two large-scale coastal protection projects, including the $300,000 effort to restore and enhance our dune system and our $25.7 million plan to upgrade the 3 miles of public seawalls surrounding our city. We are investing in our future, but we need your support.

Miami Beach needs the Federal Government to prioritize identifying economically-feasible sand sources for the continued restoration of our beaches. Since our beaches were initially restored by the U.S. Army Corps of Engineers in 1980, they have not only been instrumental in spurring our economic growth and establishing our city as one of the country's top tourist destinations, but they have also provided our investments and infrastructure with necessary storm surge protection. Recently, the offshore sand deposits that the U.S. Army Corps of Engineers depends on for the on-going maintenance of our beaches were depleted and alternative sand sources have yet to be identified. If a viable domestic source cannot be identified by the U.S. Army Corps of Engineers on-going Southeast Florida Sediment Assessment and Needs Determination (SAND) Study, the city urges that the Federal Government take the necessary steps to allow the use of non-domestic sand sources in the Dade County Beach Erosion Control and Hurricane Protection Project. Your pledge to preserve this critical asset is imperative to protect the future of our economy, our infrastructure, and our residents.

We also respectfully request your continued support of Federal agencies like the U.S. Global Change Research Program, the U.S. Geological Survey, the Federal Emergency Management Agency, and the National Oceanic and Atmospheric Administration that inform and contribute to our on-going planning and management efforts. Miami Beach is already directly engaging qualified experts and fostering cross-disciplinary dialogues with local universities such as Florida International University, Florida Atlantic University, and the University of Miami to further investigate local challenges, like the anticipated changes to our hydrology. However, U.S. communities, like Miami Beach, also depend on the data gathered by these Federal agencies to evaluate threats to public services, our infrastructure, our residents, and our industries.

Our city was the first municipality in the region to take sea level rise into consideration in stormwater management and we will continue to be at the forefront of planning for climate change and contributing to make Miami Beach and the region resilient. The city is committed to ensuring that we continue to thrive as a world-class tourist destination with a high quality of life for its residents and we are looking for your commitment to help make that happen.

Subcommittee Chairman Nelson and distinguished Subcommittee members, the City of Miami Beach would like to thank you for convening this hearing and for giving me the opportunity to testify before you. I would be pleased to answer any questions you may have.

Senator NELSON. Let me ask you on that point, so that is, what you are preparing to be ready for this October and for high tides?

Mr. LEVINE. Absolutely. Yes, sir.

Senator NELSON. And the cost of this must be enormous.

Mr. LEVINE. Senator, we are projecting the cost to be anywhere from $300 million and $400 million. Matter of fact, we have a commission meeting tomorrow, and we are going to be hopefully passing that resolution tomorrow to give the staff the go-ahead to move forward.

Senator NELSON. And you already have this in the works in anticipation of this fall.

Mr. LEVINE. We are going to be installing about three pumps for this fall, and the rest of the pumps will be in place over the next two or three years.

Senator NELSON. To what degree have you seen flooding in the streets of Miami Beach in the last couple of years?

Mr. LEVINE. It has gotten worse and worse. It is various areas. Alton Road in Miami Beach, which is a main thoroughfare, gets very flooded at certain times of the year.

The interesting thing about it, which we all know, it is no longer about rain or storm. On a beautiful sunny day, we could see our streets being flooded, which relates to what you said, with the water coming back up through our porous limestone and flooding our streets through the drains.

Senator NELSON. And is that flooding on Alton Road, is that usually connected with high tide?

Mr. LEVINE. It is connected with high tide, yes.

Senator NELSON. To what degree do the substantial summer rains add to the problem?

Mr. LEVINE. Well, that is a whole other story, and that happens as well, Senator. A lot of times during the summer rains, we won't have the proper drainage for the water to get out of our streets. So with the pumping system, which are saltwater pumps—as you said, we can't rely on gravity anymore—we are going to rely on headway of the water to be pushed out and treated and back into the bay.

Senator NELSON. Well, I want to thank you for the leadership of the City of Miami Beach.

We are going to hear from Commissioner Jacobs in a moment about the overall efforts of other jurisdictions to get in and start preparing for the future problem.

Dr. Sellers?

Dr. Sellers, did you do a spacewalk?

Mr. SELLERS. I did six, sir.

Senator NELSON. Tell everybody, to what degree do you think the views in the movie "Gravity" looked realistic?

[Laughter.]

Mr. SELLERS. Actually, sir, the views in the movie were spot-on. There was a lot of other stuff in the movie that I couldn't have agreed with, if you like, like how good-looking astronauts are.

[Laughter.]

Mr. SELLERS. But the views were right on the target, and it is a good 16 dollars' worth just to see those.

Senator NELSON. And what year were you accepted as an astronaut? In what class?

Mr. SELLERS. 1996, Sardines.

Senator NELSON. I see.

Mr. SELLERS. There were a lot of us, so they called us the Sardines.

Senator NELSON. Dr. Sellers is an example of what is called a mission specialist in the space shuttle program, usually Ph.D.s, some medical doctors, as opposed to the pilot astronauts, who are usually military test pilots and who are so accurate that they can put it on a dime. And then some of the mission specialists are also test pilots and a Ph.Ds.

So, Dr. Sellers, share with us for about five minutes.

STATEMENT OF DR. PIERS SELLERS, DEPUTY DIRECTOR, SCIENCES AND EXPLORATION DIRECTORATE, NASA GODDARD SPACE FLIGHT CENTER

Mr. SELLERS. OK. Well, good morning, Senator Nelson and citizens of Florida. It is my pleasure to appear before you today to discuss the state of science on climate change, with particular reference to global warming, sea level rise, and the likelihood of increases in the intensity of extreme weather events like hurricanes.

I would like to share with you the science community's current understanding of why the climate is changing, how it is changing, and what some of these predicted changes mean for your Floridian coastal areas. We hope this information will be useful to you for policymakers and citizens in planning for necessary adaptation and mitigation efforts.

Now, Earth Science has made some amazing advances over the last three decades, principally thanks to the data provided by a constellation of Earth-observing satellites. The view from orbit allows us to observe the whole world many times per day using a very wide spectrum of techniques and, most importantly, using a small set of well-understood, well-calibrated instruments. NASA has been at the forefront of this effort, with significant contributions provided by NOAA, USGS, and our international partners.

Now, Senator Nelson and I have both had the privilege of seeing the world from space. Space flight allows one to stand back, or float back, and take in the big picture. My take-home impression—when I say ''home,'' I mean here, Earth—is that we inhabit a very beautiful but delicate planet. And the dynamic engine of planet Earth is the climate system that allows all life here to prosper and grow, including us humans.

First of all, some facts. Over the last 150 years, the evidence from multiple archives consistently shows that surface temperatures have warmed, on average, by 0.8 degrees centigrade—that is 1½ degrees Fahrenheit—but with higher increases over land and in the northern high latitudes.

You can see the figure there. You can see the warming around the Arctic Circle and the northern continents, in particular.

Greenhouse gases from fossil-fuel burning act as a radiation-trapping blanket in the Earth's lower atmosphere and are very likely the main cause of the current global warming.

I could use some light here.

[Laughter.]

Mr. SELLERS. If I could have some light back? Thank you.

OK. Can you hear me better now?

Senator NELSON. That is much better.

Mr. SELLERS. Oh, much. Sorry about that.

Anyway, so there is the pattern of global warming over the last 100 years or so. And you can see the pattern of warming around the northern continents and the Arctic Circle in particular, warming twice as fast as the rest of the planet.

OK. The best estimate of the human contribution to this warming by our activities is close to 100 percent for the last 100 years.

So the planet is predicted to be out of energy balance, which means that more energy is coming into the system than is leaving. About 90 percent of this extra energy has been used to warm the oceans, with about seven percent to melt ice and only three percent of the energy to warm the atmosphere.

The increase in ocean heat content over the last few decades is shown in this figure. This is the top two kilometers, which is like the top mile and a half, of the global ocean; and it is the heat content, how much is being stored in the ocean. And you can see it is steadily going up over time.

Figure 3—we talked about ice melt—shows the decline in the Arctic ice sea cover over the last 35 years. And this is a satellite measurement from 1979 to now.

These changes in the flow of heat in the climate system are driving many of the other changes that we are here to talk about today. NASA's Earth Science program has a strong emphasis on understanding these changes in the global energy and water cycles using computer models and the current constellation of 17 satellites, with more planned.

Sea level can be very accurately measured by satellites, and since 1993, NASA and its partners, NOAA and the French space agency CNES, have been monitoring sea level from space.

And here you can see, sea level rise, three millimeters a year since the first measurements from space, 1993 to 2015—steady increase.

Senator NELSON. From 1993 to 2015, what is the NASA satellite measurement of total increase?

Mr. SELLERS. I could work that out for you. Boy, it is dangerous to do math on your feet, isn't it? So that is about 70 centimeters, which is about over two feet.

Sorry, correction, millimeters, which is 70 centimeters, it is about six inches or something.

Senator NELSON. Six inches.

Mr. SELLERS. Yes.

Senator NELSON. Since 1992.

Mr. SELLERS. No, wait a minute. You are asking me to do the calculation right now, and I will do it using the chart. Seventy centimeters, which is—I only think in 70 millimeters, which is 2½– 3 inches, 3 and a bit inches. Thank you. Three inches since 1993.

Senator NELSON. 1993. Just a little over two decades.

Mr. SELLERS. Yep. That is quick.

Senator NELSON. That is quick.

Mr. SELLERS. OK.

OK. In the 2014 IPCC report, there are still large uncertainties in the maximum sea level rise scenarios; that is the predicted sea level rise. But the likely range has been expanded to up to 98 centimeters, which is about three feet, by 2100. And some of our ongoing research programs are directly aimed at reducing this uncertainty.

As the global climate warms further, contributions from melting of the Greenland and Antarctic ice sheets will become more significant.

And since we are running out of time, I will just show you this figure, which shows the rate of loss of ice from Greenland to Antarctica. And you ought to really look at the sum of those, which is the right-hand bar. Different measurement techniques are shown with different colors. But that is 250 gigatons per year being lost from the ice sheets. Each gigaton is a cubic kilometer of ice, so this is an enormous ice-mass loss rate.

OK. Let's move ahead and talk about extreme weather. Predicted changes in tropical cyclone intensity is the main thing that I think is of interest to you. Calculations indicate that the mean maximum wind speed of tropical cyclones is likely to increase by up to 11 percent globally due to the projected warming. The frequency of the most intense Category 4 to 5 storms will more likely than not increase by a substantially larger percentage in some basins, including the North Atlantic.

Rainfall rates are also predicted to increase. The projected magnitude is on the order of 20 percent within 100 kilometers—that is 60 miles—of the tropical cyclone center. This increase in rainfall may increase flooding potential along the tracks of land-falling storms.

NASA has two missions, the Tropical Rainfall Monitoring Mission and the recently launched Global Precipitation Mission, to give detailed information and help us better understand the relationships between rainfall and tropical cyclone intensity.

Now, what does all this mean for Florida? By the end of the century, while an overall decrease in Atlantic tropical cyclones is expected, it is more likely than not that the frequency of Category 4 to 5 storms will increase—sorry, that is hurricanes, Category 4 to 5 hurricanes will increase. And rainfall near the centers of these hurricanes will also increase.

It is important to remember that it is the combination of a steady increase in sea level, combined with a projected increase in the rare but extreme weather events, which represents the greatest threat to Florida's coastal areas.

So, in closing, I emphasize that our ability to continuously observe changes in the global climate system, including ice sheets, sea level, and ocean characteristics—this is critical to improving our understanding of the physical processes at work.

All the data collected by NASA are made freely available to researchers and the public. Scientists at NASA and elsewhere in the U.S. and internationally are studying changes in the Earth's system as a matter of high priority in order to provide you—that is, the citizens and leaders of this country—with the best possible information with which to prepare for the future.

These sustained measurements and the supporting scientific research are critically important to improving our understanding of this planet and will allow us to better predict the phenomena associated with global climate change.

Thank you for your attention.

[The prepared statement of Mr. Sellers follows:]

PREPARED STATEMENT OF DR. PIERS SELLERS, DEPUTY DIRECTOR, SCIENCES AND EXPLORATION DIRECTORATE, NASA GODDARD SPACE FLIGHT CENTER

Chairman Nelson and Members of Congress from the state of Florida, it is my pleasure to appear before you today to discuss the state of science on climate change, with particular reference to global warming, sea level rise and the likelihood of increases in the intensity of extreme weather events. I would like to share with you the science community's current understanding of why the climate is changing, how it is changing and what some of these predicted changes mean for your coastal areas. We hope that this information will be directly useful to policy makers and citizens in setting policies and for planning necessary adaptation and mitigation efforts.

Earth science has made some amazing advances over the last three decades, principally thanks to the data provided by a constellation of Earth-observing satellites. The view from orbit allows us to observe the whole world, many times per day, using a very wide spectrum of techniques and, most importantly, using a small set of well-understood instruments. NASA has been at the forefront of this effort, with significant contributions also provided by NOAA, USGS and our international partners. These observations help us understand our planet better, and thus improve our ability to project likely future climate states, and also yield powerful societal benefits in terms of improved weather prediction, agricultural applications and water resources management, to name a few.

Senator Nelson and I have both had the privilege of seeing the world from space. Spaceflight allows one to stand back, or float, and literally take in the "big picture". My take-home impression, and when I say home, I mean here—Earth—is that we inhabit a very beautiful but delicate planet. And the dynamic engine of planet Earth is the climate system that allows all life here to prosper and grow, including us humans.

The global climate is defined as the long-term statistical behavior of the atmosphere, ocean, cryospheric and associated bio-geochemical cycles. Broadly speaking, climate is what you expect in a given year, based on long-term records and some understanding of the underlying physics, while weather, which varies from year to year, is what you actually get. Sophisticated computer models of the Earth system use satellite and other data to provide better weather forecasts. Closely related models, based on the same physical principles, are used to study the climate.

The world's climate has been observed to change over many time-scales as a result of many potential causes. Over the last 150 years,[1] the evidence from multiple archives consistently shows that surface temperatures have warmed on average by about 0.85 °C (1.6 °F),[2] but with higher increases over land and in the Northern high-latitudes, see figure 1. A wide range of studies indicate that most of this increase in temperature, and associated increases in atmospheric water vapor pressure, ocean heat content and the decreases in Arctic ice extent and mountain glaciers since 1950, at least, are very likely due to human activities.[3]

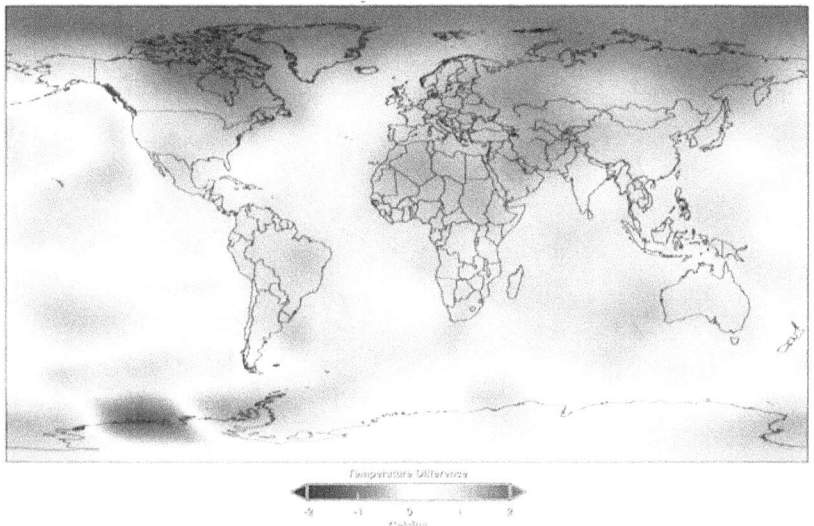

Figure 1. Color-coded map of global temperature anomalies averaged from 2008 to 2012. Reprinted from *Five Year Global Temperature Anomalies* by L. Perkins, 2013, Retrieved from *svs.gsfc.nasa.gov/vis/a000000/a004100/a004135/* and based on data from *data.giss.nasa.gov/gistemp/.*

The best estimate is that human activities have contributed close to 100 percent of the observed warming over the last 60 years or so.[4] There have been some significant natural variations (warming and cooling) in global temperature over this same period due to oscillations in the oceans and other factors, but on average these have roughly cancelled each other out. Greenhouse gases from fossil fuel burning act as a radiation-trapping blanket in the Earth's lower atmosphere and are very likely the main cause of the global warming post 1950. The evidence suggests that the most important human drivers of change are the large increases in well-mixed greenhouse gases (particularly carbon dioxide, methane, and chlorofluorocarbons) and impacts of atmospheric aerosols (sulfates, black carbon, nitrates). Smaller effects are associated with ozone changes at the surface and in the stratosphere along with land use changes (deforestation, irrigation). Natural drivers of change such as solar activity and volcanic eruptions have detectable fingerprints of change in the observations, but these changes are not large enough to appreciably add to the long-term warming.

The global climate, in simplified terms, is a response to the overall energy flow between solar forcing (heat), ocean and atmospheric heat transport and storage of this energy and the return of the energy back to space through infra-red emission.

[1] IPCC 5 Working Group 1 figure 10.5
[2] IPCC 5 Working Group 1
[3] IPCC AR5, Working Group 1 Summary for Policy Makers
[4] IPCC 5 Working Group 1

NASA's Earth Science program has a strong emphasis on understanding these changes in the global energy and water cycles using computer models and the current constellation of 17 satellites, with more planned. Given the continued increase in greenhouse gases that slow the loss of infrared energy to space, the planet is predicted to be out of energy balance—that is, more energy is coming into the system than is leaving. About 90 percent of this extra energy has been used to warm the oceans, with about 7 percent to melt ice and only 3 percent to warm the atmosphere. The increase in ocean heat content over the last few decades is shown in figure 2. This resulting net flow of heat into the climate system is driving many of the changes that we are here to talk about today.

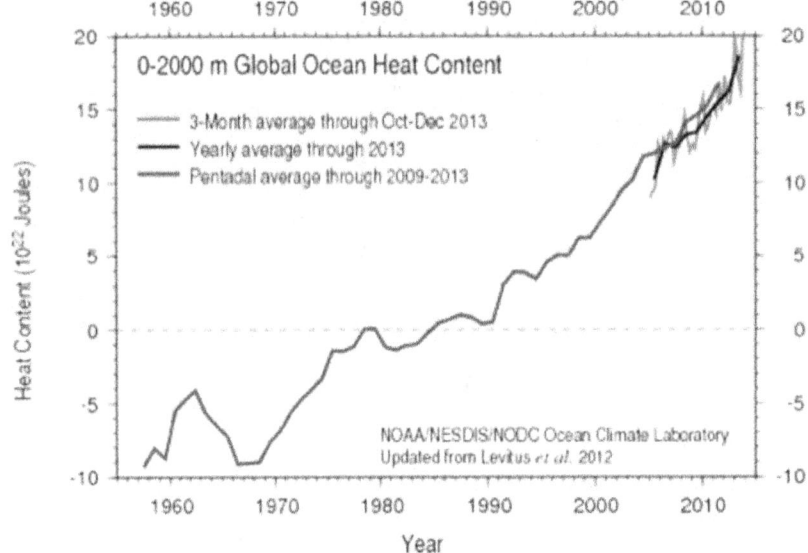

Figure 2. Global Ocean Heat Content. Reprinted from *Global Ocean Heat and Salt Content* by S. Levitus, 2012, Retrieved from *www.nodc.noaa.gov/OC5/3M\HEAT\CONTENT/*. Based on Levitus, S., J. I. Antonov, T. P. Boyer, K. Baranova, H. E. Garcia, R. A. Locarnini, A. V. Mishonov, J. R. Reagan, D. Seidov, E. S. Yarosh, and M. M. Zweng (2012), World Ocean Heat Content and thermosteric sea level change (0–2000 m), 1955–2010, *Geophys. Res. Lett., 39,* L10603, doi:10.1029/2012GL051106, 2012.

Impacts of current climate change can be seen in multiple independent datasets that come from in situ physical measurements and remote monitoring by satellite. Figure 3 shows the decline in Arctic sea ice as measured by satellite sensors over the last three decades—it can be seen that the minimum Arctic sea ice extent has significantly decreased over that time.

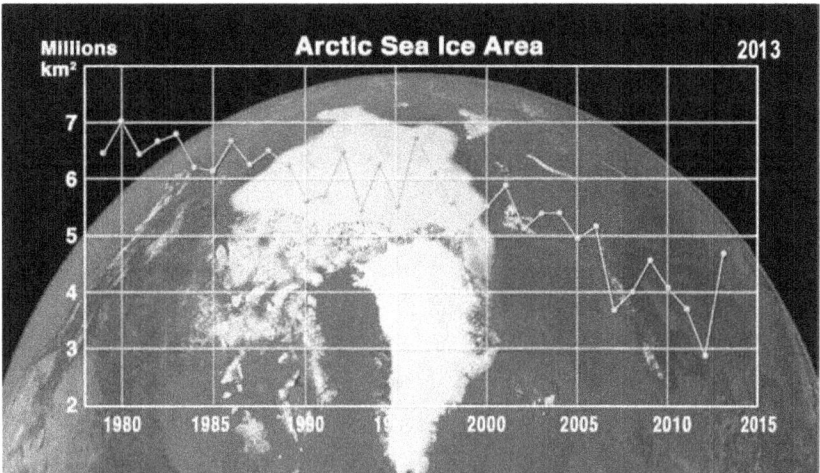

Figure 3. Annual arctic sea ice minimum from 1979 to 2013 based on satellite-based passive microwave data. Reprinted from *Annual Arctic Sea Ice Minimum 1979–2013 with Area Graph* by C.Starr, 2013, Retrieved from *svs.gsfc.nasa.gov/vis/a000000/a004100/a004131/*

Sea level can be very accurately measured by satellites and since 1993 NASA and its partners, principally NOAA and the French space agency CNES, have been monitoring sea level continuously from space using satellite altimetry missions including Topex/Poseidon, Jason 1 and Jason 2 over this time period. Future missions include Jason-3 (launching in 2015) and the Surface Water Ocean Topography (SWOT) mission. Tide gauges provide independent assessments of altimeter data and provide region-specific information. These in situ data inform local projections that can differ from the global picture because of local ground movements and regional ocean currents. Figure 4 shows the measured rise in sea level from these satellite data sources.

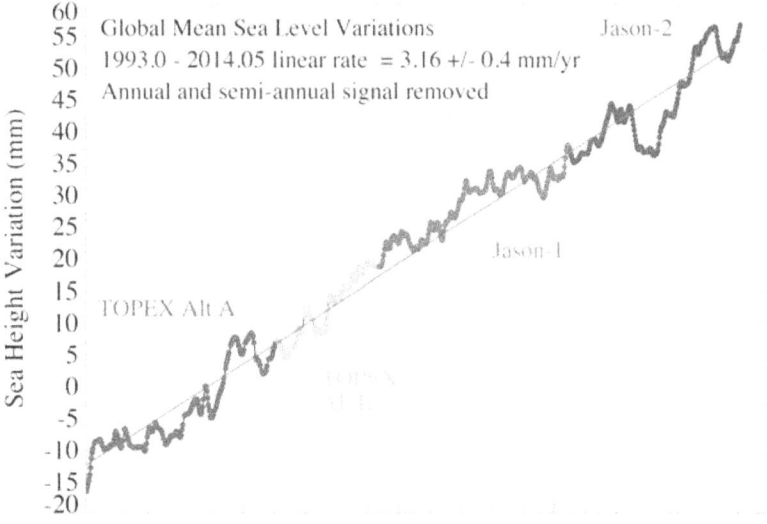

Figure 4. Global mean sea level rise based on data from satellite altimetry.

It can be seen that global sea level has increased by over 3 mm/year over the last 20 years. Projections of the expected increase in sea level rise over the 21st century have also been raised as we have learned more about ice sheets, groundwater changes and ocean heating, see figure 5.

The 2007 Intergovernmental Panel on Climate Change (IPCC) report was unable to give a range for the contribution of ice sheet melt to sea level rise (but suggested that other terms would lead to a maximum of 59 cm by 2100). In the 2014 IPCC report, there are still large uncertainties in the maximum scenarios, but the "likely" range has been expanded to up to 98 cm.[5] Some of NASA's ongoing research programs are directly aimed at reducing this uncertainty.

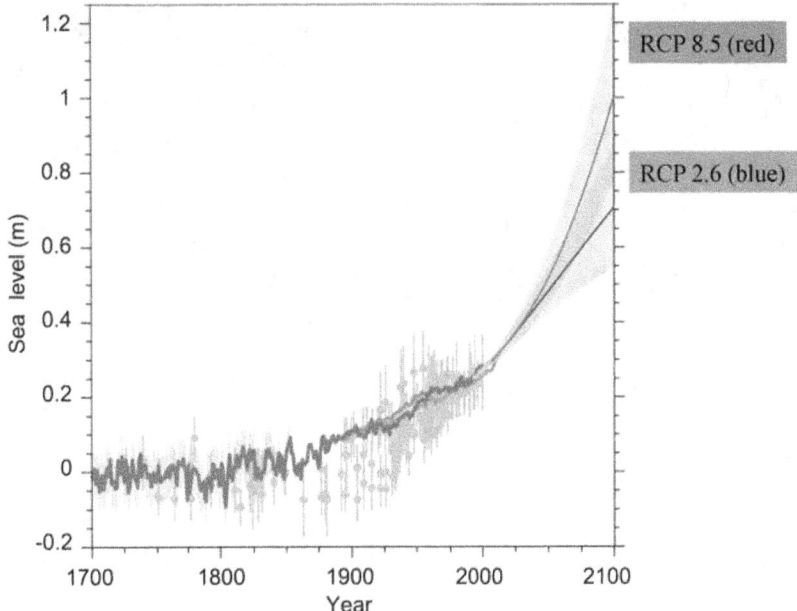

Figure 5. Compilation of paleo sea level data, tide gauge data, altimeter data, and central estimates and likely ranges for projections of global mean sea level rise for *RCP2.6 (blue)* and *RCP8.5 (red)* scenarios, all relative to pre-industrial values. From Church, J.A., P.U. Clark, A. Cazenave, J.M. Gregory, S. Jevrejeva, A. Levermann, M.A. Merrifield, G.A. Milne, R.S. Nerem, P.D. Nunn, A.J. Payne, W.T. Pfeffer, D. Stammer and A.S. Unnikrishnan, 2013: Sea Level Change. In: *Climate Change 2013: The Physical Science Basis. Contribution of Working Group I to the Fifth Assessment Report of the Intergovernmental Panel on Climate Change* [Stocker, T.F., D. Qin, G.-K. Plattner, M. Tignor, S.K. Allen, J. Boschung, A. Nauels, Y. Xia, V. Bex and P.M. Midgley (eds.)]. Cambridge University Press, Cambridge, United Kingdom and New York, NY, USA.

The principal factors that affect global sea level are ocean temperature, ice volume, and tectonic activity. Over short, decadal and centennial, time scales, sea level is most influenced by temperature and ice volume changes. Currently, most of the change in global sea level is the result of increases in ocean heat content as the ocean expands very slightly as it warms. The melting of glaciers is estimated to have contributed about one third of the observed sea level rise shown in figure 4. As the global climate warms further, contributions from melting of the Greenland and Antarctic ice sheets will become more significant. Both ice sheets have lost ice at an increasing rate since the 1990s. In particular, Gravity Recovery and Climate Experiment (GRACE) satellites that can measure small variations in the Earth's gravity field from space show that significant amounts of ice sheet and glacier melting are occurring in Greenland, Alaska and West Antarctica. Figure 6 shows the latest estimates of the annual decrease in the mass of the Earth's major ice sheets, derived using four independent data sources over the last few decades.

---

[5] IPCC AR5 Working Group 1

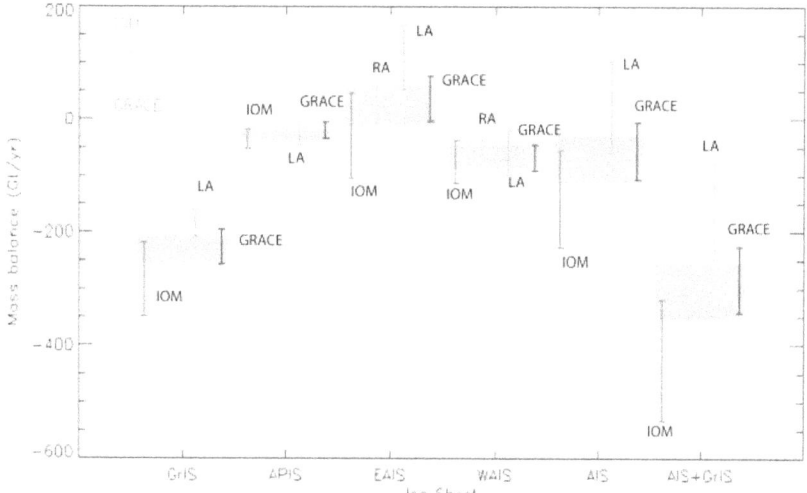

Figure 6. Intercomparisons of ice mass balance estimates using four independent geodetic techniques: Input-Output Method (IOM), red), Radar Altimetry (RA, cyan), Laser Altimetry (LA, green), and gravimetry (GRACE, blue). Four regional areas are considered: the Greenland Ice Sheet (GrIS), Antarctic Peninsula Ice Sheet (APIS), East Antarctic Ice Sheet (EAIS), West Antarctic Ice Sheet (WAIS), the combined Antarctic Ice Sheet (AIS), and the overall estimate for the AIS and GrIS. The grey areas constitute the reconciled estimates. From Shepherd, A., *et al., A Reconciled Estimate of Ice Sheet Mass Balance,* Science, 2012

With the development of satellite and airborne remote sensing capabilities, coupled with improved field measurements and modeling efforts, we are beginning to understand current changes and gain insights into what the future may hold for the Greenland and Antarctic ice sheets. Our satellite and airborne capabilities are providing observations of glacier flow rates, ice topography (which is indicative of the underlying processes that affect change), mass change, and depth and topography of the bedrock that lies beneath the ice. This last point is particularly important because the geometry of the bed, in conjunction with surface elevations, largely determines the extent to which glaciers will continue to accelerate or will slow down.

Current and planned investments in missions such as the Ice, Cloud and Land Elevation Satellite 2 (ICESat-2—measuring ice elevation change) and the Gravity Recovery and Climate Experiment (GRACE) follow-on measuring ice mass change) and airborne observations of ice topography and glacier bed geometries provide insights into the underlying mechanisms of ice sheet changes. Space geodesy, satellite and airborne radars all provide more information that helps to pin down details related to glacier motion and ice sheet changes. NASA also works with data from its international partners to examine the variations in flow rates of outlet glaciers, tracking the magnitude and character of their acceleration. The information gained from all of these projects is incorporated into ice sheet models designed to predict how ice sheets will contribute to sea level rise in the next one or two centuries. The modeling activity is an integrated effort jointly carried out by NASA, the National Science Foundation, and the Department of Energy (DOE). NSF also invests in basic observations and process studies that are either directly coordinated with or are complementary to NASA's activities, and DOE is building dynamical models of Greenland and Antarctica, where future sea level rise projections take advantage of observations provided by NASA and NSF.

Sustained observations of ocean elevation from satellites combined with tide gauges will provide continuous measurements of sea level rise. Current and planned observations of ice sheets and glaciers will provide necessary insights into the physical processes that govern their contributions to sea level rise. Ongoing and planned measurements of ocean characteristics will continue to inform our assessments of temperature and circulation characteristics, which affect the rate of expansion. Continued observations of the movement of water throughout the Earth will provide important insights into the characteristics of land-water storage. All of these data are critical inputs used to inform models and improve our understanding of the physics, carrying us closer to a more complete and robust sea level rise prediction.

The net flow of heat into the climate system that I referred to earlier is likely to affect the intensity and frequency of extreme weather events in many parts of the globe. Our ability to predict changes in the likelihood of these events is so far relatively limited but intensive research continues in this important area. The most recent report of the International Panel on Climate Change (IPCC 5) states that it is likely that the global *frequency* of tropical cyclones will either decrease or remain essentially unchanged owing to greenhouse warming. These findings speak directly to tropical cyclones, not other severe weather events. Projected decreases in tropical cyclone frequency appear to be related to a weakening of the tropical circulation associated with a decrease in the upward mass flux in regions of deep convection under global warming. However, there is lower confidence associated with these projections.

The predicted change in storm intensity is a different story-and one we can speak to with greater confidence. Calculations indicate that the mean maximum wind speed of tropical cyclones is likely to increase by +2 to +11 percent globally due to the projected twenty-first-century warming, although increases may not occur in all tropical regions. Two studies referred to in the latest IPCC report project near-term increases of North Atlantic hurricane intensity driven in large part by projected reductions in tropospheric aerosols. The frequency of the most intense Category 4 and 5 storms will more likely than not increase by a substantially larger percentage in some basins, including the North Atlantic. For the North Atlantic, an estimate of the time scale of observed emergence of projected changes in intense tropical cyclone frequency is longer than 60 years. This is because these are relatively rare events and getting a statistically significant sample takes time.

NASA's Hurricane and Severe Storm Sentinel (HS3) mission is delivering important information that will improve our ability to predict the track and intensity of hurricanes as well as provide information related to how hurricanes may intensify in a warming world. HS3 uses two Global Hawk unmanned aerial vehicles to fly around and over storms developing in the Atlantic. The Global Hawks are capable of extended missions, 24 hours or longer, and make multiple passes over the developing storms, tracking the wind and convective processes that lead to a storm's intensification or weakening. As sea levels rise, enhanced understanding of hurricanes and their potential intensities and tracks will become ever more important.

Rainfall rates associated with storms are likely to increase. The projected magnitude is on the order of +20 percent within 100 km of the tropical cyclone center. The increase in rainfall rates associated with tropical cyclones is a consistent feature of the numerical models projecting greenhouse warming as atmospheric moisture content in the tropics and tropical cyclone moisture convergence is projected to increase. This increase in rainfall may increase flooding potential along the tracks of land-falling storms. Resulting changes to water vapor pathways and the dynamical pattern of the troposphere may lead to increased coastal rainfall and drying continental interiors. NASA's Tropical Rainfall Measuring Mission (TRMM) and the recently launched Global Precipitation Mission (GPM) are providing detailed information to help better understand relationships between rainfall and tropical cyclone intensity, and how tropical cyclones and extreme weather events can affect the U.S. and regions around the world.

There is low confidence in projected changes in tropical cyclone genesis location, storm tracks, duration, and areas of impact. Existing model projections do not show dramatic large-scale changes in these features. However, the vulnerability of coastal regions to storm-surge flooding is expected to increase with future sea-level rise and coastal development, although this vulnerability will also depend on future storm characteristics.

What does all of this mean for Florida? By the end of the century, the intensity of hurricanes, including rainfall near the centers of hurricanes, may increase. It is not currently possible to determine whether the number of hurricanes impacting Florida will change. But even if hurricane frequency and intensity do not change, rising sea levels and coastal development *will likely increase the impact* of hurricanes and other coastal storms on those coastal communities and infrastructure. It is important to remember that it is the combination of a steady increase in sea level combined with a projected increase in rare but extreme weather events which represents the greatest threat to Florida's coastal areas.

In closing, I emphasize that our ability to continuously observe changes in the global climate system, including ice sheets, sea level, and ocean characteristics, is critical to improving our understanding of the physical processes at work. All the data collected by NASA are made freely available to researchers and the public. Scientists in NASA and elsewhere in the U.S. and internationally are studying changes in the Earth's system as a matter of high priority in order to provide you—the citizens and leaders of this country—with the best possible information with which to prepare for the future. These sustained measurements and the supporting scientific research are critically important to improving our understanding of this planet and will allow us to better predict the phenomena associated with global climate change.

Senator NELSON. Dr. Sellers, I think it is——

[Applause.]

Senator NELSON. I think it is important to point out that Dr. Sellers? testimony is not modeling, is not a forecast, it is a measurement. What he has stated, in fact, has occurred. And so those who deny climate change and sea level rise, here is the proof right here.

Now, in one projection that he had toward the year 2100, three feet? Does everybody here know what that would do to the State of Florida and the 75 percent of the state's population that is along the coast? And that is less than a century away. And it doesn't happen all at once in the year 2100. It is happening right now.

Dr. Sellers, thank you very, very much.

Mr. SELLERS. Thank you.

[Applause.]

Senator NELSON. OK. Commissioner Jacobs, please.

STATEMENT OF KRISTIN JACOBS, COUNTY COMMISSIONER, BROWARD COUNTY, FLORIDA; MEMBER, WHITE HOUSE TASK FORCE ON CLIMATE PREPAREDNESS AND RESILIENCE

Ms. JACOBS. Well, Senator, I have to first thank you so much for convening this hearing today. As we have heard, the issues facing South Florida are huge and they are long-term, and this means that we need to act now.

As you know, here in South Florida we are close to making the community understand that this isn't magic that we are talking about, this is science. And science is predictable, and there are measures that we can take to address it.

During my years as a Broward County commissioner, I devoted a great deal of time and effort and passion to the issue of climate change. And the more that I learned, the more that I realized that these issues weren't just affecting Broward County; in fact, it was affecting our sister counties, Miami-Dade, Palm Beach, and Monroe Counties. We were all pretty much in the same situation. We were all addressing climate change, perhaps a little bit differently from one another.

And it drew our attention to the fact that the scale of this problem facing us meant that we were going to have to learn to work together, we were going to have to find a way to come together across those human-imposed boundaries of our communities, because of course water and hurricanes and other natural phenomena don't respect these boundaries, and that we needed to also do this across party lines, which is, I think, one of the most significant things about what the four counties did in coming together and signing a historic compact. This fall will make five years since that compact was signed. We are still the only counties in the Nation to have come together in such a way.

And I think the issue of party is particularly important when you consider that when the saltwater has overtopped your seawall and filled up your swimming pool or your sewers are backing up into your home, do you really care what party it is that the person is from who answers the phone? No, we don't, we want answers. And we expect our government to be acting proactively.

So I am thrilled to have this panel and this opportunity to talk about what is happening to the 5.5 million residents of the four counties and these new heights of cooperation that we have begun and embracing this regional approach to resiliency.

I would first like to begin with some of what we have heard today, the doom and gloom that is facing the region. But mostly what I would like to end up with is to talk about why I believe there is reason for calm optimism, because it isn't all bad news.

The sobering truth, though, is that Broward County and the South Florida region are facing significant vulnerabilities. As we have already heard this morning, they go from coastal and inland flooding, ''inland'' being an operative word. We talk a lot about coastal flooding, but it is important to understand what happens on the coast affects areas inland, in many cases even greater than what we may see on the coast—storm surge, saltwater contamination of our drinking water supplies is greatly threatened, the impacts to our wastewater systems was spoken of a little bit earlier, beach erosion, and the threats to the public and private property infrastructure alone.

We are also going to be experiencing hotter temperatures, public health challenges, ocean acidification, and additional stresses to the Everglades. Many of these impacts will affect critical resources, community sustainability, and the very heart of our economic engine, that of tourism.

Sea level rise is just one result of climate change, but the challenges we are facing from this one issue paint a daunting picture. To give you an idea of the scope of the issue for Palm Beach, Broward, and Monroe Counties, at just one foot of sea level rise, up to $4 billion of taxable property will be inundated with seawater. And this figure does not include Miami-Dade County. At three feet, that figure rises to $31 billion.

Keep in mind that a significant percentage of our sewer systems, as we have talked about, is gravity-fed. That means waste literally rolls downhill. And without the infrastructure for pumps to move it, we have some huge costs ahead of us.

Sea level rise also affects our drinking water. As saltwater migrates inland into the freshwater aquifer, we will lose our freshwater wells. In Broward County alone, that saltwater intrusion line continues to march ever inland. In the City of Fort Lauderdale, it is about six miles in, to give you an idea. Everything on the other side of that saltwater line, all those water wells have been lost.

As we have talked about this issue across the four counties, it is important to understand that in Broward County there are 28 water utilities. So when you lose your wells, you have to go to the next municipality, which may not be able to deliver water to your region.

So we know and we have heard a lot today about all of the different problems facing us as a community, but what I wanted to spend some time today to talk to you about was what is happening as a part of the compact.

Through the counties agreeing to come together, we adopted 110 specific recommendations on climate change. Unprecedented that you would take these very controversial issues, 110 recommendations, and have 4 county governments adopt them. These recommendations spanned seven different topics, from energy, water, transportation, sustainable communities, natural systems, agriculture, and outreach and public policy.

So with the Climate Action Plan, we understood that within the four counties there are more than 100 cities, that they all needed to address this in their own ways. But we also understood very pragmatically that when we pull together in the same direction, we could share not only our financial resources but our staff resources as well.

The other interesting point about moving together in the same direction is the counties and the cities have learned how to not compete with one another. And I would use Miami Beach as an example, where you had multiple counties going after a grant who all decided to stand back, instead support one city in their bid for a grant, which they were awarded. In the past, we might all have had our hands out, all fighting over that limited pot of dollars. We have rightly understood that working together really will advance the cause of solutions for the region.

And while all of this gives us a great reason to celebrate success—and I won't go into all the different ways in which we have made changes within our communities—we couldn't have gotten here if it weren't for our Federal partners.

The Federal partners, particularly between NOAA and USGS, helped the four counties baseline our science, which sounds like an easy task until you get four counties' worth of scientists in the room who are all pretty married to their projections. It took us about a year to get us all on the same page. But that helped us understand how we could then go in and make other changes that would pull us in the same direction and also help us to speak with one voice.

The other Federal agencies—it isn't just USGS and NOAA, but the Department of Energy, the Army Corps, the Federal Highway Administration all have given us their resources.

We look forward to a time where the Federal Government, who is already spending money in our communities and throughout this country, will start to tie climate change resiliency—start to tie funding to the communities' ability to recognize and prioritize where their vulnerabilities are. Those dollars that are already being spent can be spent more wisely. And while we do need huge infusions of new cash, we know that using the dollars that we have now more wisely will benefit us all.

Our President, through the creation of this task force, the Climate Preparedness and Resilience Task Force, has drawn together governors, mayors, and local commissioners from all over the country to craft recommendations so that the Federal Government can be even more responsive to us. We are so impressed and proud of what our President is doing in rightly understanding the challenges and that local governments are already in the trenches moving us forward.

But, Senator Nelson, it is truly a pleasure to be here with you today to understand that it isn't just our President that understands these pressures and how the Federal Government can come and be a resource to us, but you, in holding this committee today, have understood, as my mother always said, that if you are not at the table, you are on the menu.

[Laughter.]

Ms. JACOBS. And so today I just have to tell you how much we appreciate sitting at your table today to be able to be part of the solution and also to help guide in any way that you need us to get your back and making sure that the rest of the Senate and the U.S. House of Representatives understand this important issue not just to South Florida but the entire United States.

[The prepared statement of Ms. Jacobs follows:]

PREPARED STATEMENT OF KRISTIN JACOBS, COUNTY COMMISSIONER, BROWARD COUNTY, FLORIDA; MEMBER, WHITE HOUSE TASK FORCE ON CLIMATE PREPAREDNESS AND RESILIENCE

Good Morning Mr. Chairman,

I would like to personally thank you for your leadership and for convening this hearing today in South Florida.

As you know, Florida, and especially South Florida, is vulnerable to the effects of Climate Change.

During my public service as a Broward County Commissioner, I have devoted a great amount of effort—and passion—to addressing Climate Change. And the more I learned, the more I realized that the issues facing my county were the same issues facing my sister counties here in South Florida. The scale of the need for comprehensive responses and pragmatic solutions meant that we were going to have to think like Mother Nature does: regionally, holistically, and long term. From that idea began a four-county effort committed to working across the human-imposed boundaries of cities and counties. We also faced the significant journey of working beyond party lines. After all, when saltwater has overtopped the seawall and filled your swimming pool, or sewer water is backing up in your house, do you care which party the person you call for answers belongs?

I am thrilled to be before this esteemed panel today to share with you the exciting ways our super region, one which represents 5.5 million people has worked together to reach new heights of coordination and cooperation by embracing a regional approach to resiliency.

I would first like to begin with what some might term as the "doom and gloom" outlook we are facing, and then share with you why I believe there is good reason for calm optimism.

The sobering truth is that Broward County and the South Florida region are facing significant vulnerabilities. They include:

- Coastal and inland flooding
- Storm surge
- Saltwater contamination of drinking water supplies
- Impacts to water supply and wastewater systems
- Beach erosion
- Threats to public and private property and infrastructure.

We will also experience:

- Hotter temperatures
- Public health challenges
- Ocean acidification and warming with impacts to coral reefs and fisheries
- Additional stresses on the Everglades.

Many of these impacts will affect critical resources, community sustainability, and the heart of our economic engine—tourism.

Sea level rise is just one result of Climate Change, but the challenges we are facing from this one issue alone paint a daunting picture. To give you an idea of the scope of the issue for Palm Beach, Broward, and Monroe counties, at just one foot of sea level rise up to $4 billion of taxable property will be inundated with seawater. That number does not even include Miami-Dade County. At three feet, that figure rises to $31 billion. Keep in mind that a significant percentage of our sewer systems are gravity-fed, meaning that waste literally rolls downhill. These figures do not take into account the inland impacts that would take hold when these non-pump-operated systems begin to fail.

Sea level rise also affects our drinkable water, as salt water migrates inland into the fresh water aquifer; we lose our fresh water wells. The salt water intrusion line in Broward County has been creeping steadily west. As that salt water intrusion line marches ever westward and we lose more and more wells, local governments will have to seek water from new sources. Local governments may look to the nearest utility, but there is no guarantee the infrastructure required to provide water to so many new customers will exist. This situation will pose great difficulty for local governments.

It is especially daunting for Broward County, when you consider that unlike Miami-Dade County, which has a large water utility, Broward has 28 separate individually governed water utilities supplying 31 cities. The cost of reaching inland to compensate for loss of wells in the coastal zone is estimated to be upwards of $350 million in Broward County alone.

Restoring the Everglades must remain a high priority at all levels of government, not only for the value of maintaining a unique ecosystem, but also because restored freshwater flow through the Everglades system will help protect drinking water supplies threatened by sea level rise.

Sea level rise also increases the severity of flooding and makes drainage more expensive. Broward County consists of 1,800 linear miles of canals and myriad retention lakes all connected and designed to keep us dry. Most people do not know that the urbanized area of Broward accounts for only one-third of the actual acreage in our county. The other two-thirds are held in conservation land, our beautiful and one-of-a-kind Everglades. The Everglades has a higher elevation than the urbanized area and the cost of pumping and maintaining water levels continues to escalate.

Here are few other examples from the region.

Fort Lauderdale recently estimated that it might cost $1 billion to upgrade the city's storm water system in the face of rising sea levels and increased flooding. Miami Beach pegged its storm water upgrades at $400 million. Pumps to replace gravity water control structures are estimated at $50 million each. This doesn't speak to the improvements needed within associated drainage basins, or improvements to roadways and other infrastructure. There's no question that these are large numbers. These examples show that these issues are not limited to just one city or county.

Now the reasons for my optimism.

In 2009 Broward, Palm Beach, Miami-Dade and Monroe Counties came together to form the Southeast Florida Regional Climate Change Compact. I am proud to say that we have been able to work together on an agreement to reduce greenhouse gas emissions and to adapt to climate change impacts we are already living with.

While we have been recognized both nationally and internationally as a leading example of effective local climate action, I am most proud of the work the staff of each county has done in putting together our Regional Climate Action Plan covering 110 specific recommendations for resiliency divided into seven categories:

1. Energy
2. Water
3. Transportation
4. Sustainable Communities
5. Natural Systems
6. Agriculture
7. Outreach and Public Policy

While the Regional Climate Action Plan leaves it up the individual counties and cities to implement the plan in the ways which works best for them, we are finding that in practice, it makes fiscal and practical sense to work together. It is this spirit of cooperation, the ability to share and learn from each other, which has led to accelerated action throughout our region.

Examples of what we have seen so far include:

• Incorporation of climate change considerations into county comprehensive plans and other planning documents,

• Efforts to advance a regional surface water reservoir providing water supply benefits for communities in Palm Beach, Broward and Miami-Dade counties by improving surface water storage, diversion of storm water runoff and aquifer recharge.

- The formation of a coastal resilience work group to expand the use of coral reefs, mangroves, dunes and other living shoreline projects. When integrated with urban systems, these provide optimum shoreline protection, habitat preservation, or restoration.

And while all of this gives us great reason to celebrate success, the truth is, we could not have done it without our Federal partners.

- Agencies like NOAA and USGS helped the four counties baseline our projections for how high the sea will rise and by when so we are all working from the same set of assumptions.
- A grant from NOAA is enabling Broward County, the South Florida Regional Planning Council and the City of Fort Lauderdale to explore the use of "Adaptation Action Areas." A recent innovation in Florida law that allows communities to identify climate-vulnerable areas and prioritize where adaptation investments should go first.
- The Regional Climate Action Plan mitigation priorities include mitigation and programs like the Go Solar Florida program which is funded by a U.S. Department of Energy Grant. This program makes installing rooftop solar easier and more affordable for homeowners.
- Broward and Miami-Dade counties have worked with the U.S. Geological Survey to create advanced hydrologic models that look at the interaction between sea level rise, stormwater and potable water supply.
- Compact Partners are benefiting from a Federal Highway Administration grant to assess the vulnerability of transportation infrastructure to climate change.

Local governments and regional initiatives like the Compact play a significant role in supporting regional decision making with technical support, expertise, and financial assistance from the Federal Government.

Although the local level is where much of the needed adaptation to climate impacts will happen, we are still in great need of policies at the state, Federal and international levels that reduce carbon pollution and accelerate the transition to a clean energy economy.

I have the personal honor and privilege of serving on President Obama's State, Local and Tribal Leaders Task Force on Climate Preparedness and Resilience. I remain immensely impressed with our President's consistent recognition that local governments are already in the trenches dealing with the impacts of climate change and that we have common sense solutions to offer.

Our President, through the creation of this Task Force, has drawn together governors, mayors and county commissioners from all over the country to craft recommendations to help the Federal Government understand exactly what they what we need in order to become prepared for and resilient to the effects of a changing climate, whether its drought, or flood, or fire or hurricanes or mudslides.

Senators, I must tell you that it is not only impressive that our President is listening and reaching out to us, but so too, are you. You have rightly recognized that, as my mom used to quip, "If you're not at the table, you're on the menu."

On behalf of the entire Broward County Commission and our sister Counties, Miami-Dade, Palm Beach and Monroe, and more than 100 cities in the South Florida region, I thank you for the opportunity to sit at your table today and share my insights.

Southeast Florida Regional Climate Change Compact

WHEREAS, there is consensus among the world's leading scientists that global climate change is among the most significant problems facing the world today; and

WHEREAS, Florida is considered one of the most vulnerable areas in the country to the consequences of climate change with Southeast Florida on the front line to experience the impacts of climate change, especially sea level rise; and

WHEREAS, Broward, Miami-Dade, Palm Beach and Monroe Counties, herein the four counties that constitute the Southeast Florida Region, share in common a strong quality of life rooted in the region's rich cultural heritage, vigorous economy, and environmental resources of global significance; and

WHEREAS, the aforementioned four counties of Southeast Florida, which represent approximately 30 percent of the population of the State of Florida, are physically linked one to the other by the Atlantic Ocean coastline and share some of the world's most renowned natural resources such as the Everglades, our unique coral reefs, beautiful beaches, and fragile Keys ecosystem; and

WHEREAS, the four counties of Southeast Florida and their respective populations, totaling more than five million residents, are expected to share in disproportionately high risks associated with climate change due to low land elevations, rising sea level projections, and anticipated increases in tropical storm events; and

WHEREAS, rising sea levels could limit the effectiveness of critical drainage infrastructure, endanger beaches, and coastal natural resources and increase incidents of saltwater intrusion on the Biscayne Aquifer—putting at risk the drinking water supply for the entire population of Southeast Florida; and

WHEREAS, local governments, and the region as a whole, must give significant consideration to adaptation strategies designed to protect public infrastructure, property, water resources, natural areas and native species, and basic quality of life; and

WHEREAS, the aforementioned four counties of Southeast Florida account for a combined Gross Domestic Product of more than $2.5 billion annually and more than 37 percent of statewide economic output; and

WHEREAS, while the four counties of Southeast Florida have independently taken steps to address global climate change, all parties recognize that coordinated and collective action on this, the defining issue for Southeast Florida in the 21st Century, will best serve the citizens of the region;

NOW THEREFORE, BE IT RESOLVED BY THE BOARDS OF COUNTY COMMISSIONERS OF THE FOUR COUNTIES OF SOUTHEAST FLORIDA:

SECTION 1: That each county shall work in close collaboration with the aforementioned counties of Southeast Florida party to this compact to develop a joint policy position urging the United States Congress to pass legislation that recognizes the unique vulnerabilities of Southeast Florida to the impacts of climate change and to further a joint policy position that includes specific recommendations regarding the allocation of Federal climate change funding based on vulnerability to climate change impacts. Such recommendations might include designation of areas of Southeast Florida as uniquely vulnerable and of Federal interest for the purpose of securing enhanced levels of Federal participation in regional adaptation projects.

SECTION 2: That each county shall work in close collaboration with the other counties party to this compact to develop additional legislative policy statements relating to global climate change and future legislation to be considered by the Congress of the United States for transmittal to the Congressional Delegation representing, in part or in whole, districts within the area covered by this compact.

SECTION 3: That each county shall work in close collaboration with other counties party to this compact in developing joint position statements on proposed State legislation and energy/climate policies including but not limited to issues such as the region's energy and climate security and a renewable energy portfolio standard that defines renewable energy sources as wind, solar, geothermal, biomass, landfill gas, qualified hydropower, and marine and hydrokinetic energy, and also including nuclear energy, and to collaborate on other emerging energy/climate issues that may be considered by the 2010 Florida Legislature for transmittal to the Legislative Delegation representing, in part or in whole, districts within the area covered by this compact.

SECTION 4: That each county shall work with other counties party to this compact in developing joint position statements for future State legislation that may be considered by the Florida Legislature for transmittal to the Legislative Delegation representing, in part or in whole, districts within the area covered by this compact.

SECTION 5: That each county shall commit appropriate staff resources and expertise, within budget constraints, to participate in a Regional Climate Team with other counties party to this compact toward the development of a Southeast Florida Regional Climate Change Action Plan.

SECTION 6: That each county shall work with other counties party to this compact in developing a Southeast Florida Regional Climate Change Action Plan, understanding that no county will work at cross-purposes with the other counties. The Action Plan could, at a minimum, include the following components:

- A baseline of greenhouse gas emissions for Southeast Florida;
- Strategies for coordinated emission reductions throughout the built environment to include the use of energy efficiency, energy conservation, and the use of demand-side renewable energy resources;
- Strategies for coordinated emission reductions from the transportation sector to include increased reliance on public transit, emerging vehicle technologies, and advanced biofuels;
- Strategies for coordinated emission reductions resulting from changes in local and regional land use;
- Strategies for the coordinated regional preparation for and adaptation to a rapidly changing global environment based upon regional mapping of projected sea-level rise and any resulting amplification of localized impacts of tropical cyclone events. Such strategies shall incorporate climate preparation concerns for the regional economy, regional infrastructure and the built environment, social and cultural needs, and natural systems within the four counties party to this compact.

SECTION 7: That each county shall commit to participating with other counties party to this compact in hosting the Second Southeast Florida Regional Climate Change Summit in October, 2010.

BR⊗WARD
COUNTY
F L O R I D A
Adopted December 8, 2009

MIAMI-DADE
COUNTY
Adopted December 1, 2009

Adopted January 20, 2010**

Adopted December 15, 2009

*City of Key West: Resolution of support for the Compact – December 15, 2009

** Second adoption date following minor changes made by partnering Counties

---

SOUTHEAST FLORIDA REGIONAL CLIMATE CHANGE COMPACT COUNTIES

2014 FEDERAL ENERGY AND CLIMATE LEGISLATIVE PROGRAM

Background

Southeast Florida is one of the most vulnerable areas in the country to climate change and sea level rise. Recognizing their shared challenges, Palm Beach, Broward, Miami-Dade and Monroe counties (Compact counties) adopted the Southeast Florida Regional Climate Change Compact (Compact) in 2010. The Compact includes a commitment to develop and advocate for joint state and Federal legislative policies. Therefore, the Compact counties have adopted a *Federal Energy and Climate Legislative Program* each year since 2011.

The following Federal policies and priorities form the *Southeast Florida Regional Climate Change Compact Counties 2014 Federal Energy and Climate Legislative Program:*

Infrastructure Investments

SUPPORT—the Water Resources Reform and Development Act of 2013 (WRRDA) and specific support for provisions:

- Authorizing Everglades restoration projects, either by name or by reference to those projects for which Chief's Reports have been completed.
- Creating a procedure for later authorization of projects under review at the time of passage of the Act, such as the Central Everglades Planning Project.
- Allowing non-federal sponsors to receive reimbursement or in-kind credit for project expenditures incurred before the execution of a Project Partnership Agreement with the Army Corps of Engineers.
- Creating an evaluation procedure for Federal shore protection projects nearing the end of their 50-year Federal authorization and allowing the Assistant Secretary of the Army to extend the authorization for an additional 15 years.
- Supporting the potential use of nonstructural alternatives, such as dunes, wetlands, marshes, reefs, mangroves, and other natural features.
- Creating a Water Infrastructure Finance and Innovation Authority (WIFIA).

SUPPORT—federal legislation that would create and fund a national infrastructure bank or other new infrastructure funding source to finance projects needed by state and local governments to adapt to climate impacts and address aging infrastructure. Emphasis should be placed on investments in water management, water supply, transportation, and other projects that make urban infrastructure more resilient to extreme weather events and rising sea levels.

SUPPORT—legislation that creates incentives for the consideration of climate impacts, including sea level rise, in Federal aid for transportation, water, and other infrastructure projects.

SUPPORT—the use of emissions reduction and climate adaptation performance measures and standards to evaluate infrastructure investments, including transportation and water projects.

SUPPORT—federal programs that shift priorities toward public transit and non-motorized travel, including reinvestment in existing infrastructure and communities, support for public transportation and transit-oriented development, and congestion management strategies other than new road building.

Adaptation and Resilience

SUPPORT—Congressional recognition of adaptation as a critical climate change issue in the development of all legislation and appropriations priorities.

SUPPORT—specific recognition in Federal legislation of land use designations made by local governments for the purposes of building community resilience, such as the Adaptation Action Areas (AAAs) defined in Chapter 163, Florida Statutes, and the development of regulations that give priority consideration to local land use designations for climate-resilient investments.

SUPPORT—federal grants, technical support, and other services to aid community planning that incorporates sustainability and climate adaptation practices.

SUPPORT—reform of the Stafford Act to allow greater flexibility in disaster reconstruction efforts to ensure that properties and infrastructure are not merely rebuilt to their previous condition, but to higher, more resilient standards (where appropriate).

SUPPORT—funding for weatherization programs provided by the U.S. Department of Energy to harden buildings against windstorm impacts.

SUPPORT—continued funding for the Federal Emergency Management Administration's (FEMA) natural hazard mitigation programs to include mitigation for hazards associated with climate change impacts.

SUPPORT—the continued eligibility of funding for activities to adapt to climate change and extreme weather events under the Federal-Aid and Federal Lands Highway programs, including vulnerability/risk assessments, highway project development, environmental review and design, construction of projects or features to protect existing assets, and evaluation of life cycle costs.

Program Cuts and Restrictions

OPPOSE—reduction in funding for critically important conservation, public health, and environmental protection efforts that reduce carbon emissions, support climate preparedness, build resilience to extreme weather, and protect the Nation's natural resources.

Climate and Energy Research

SUPPORT—creation of a National Climate Service within the National Oceanic and Atmospheric Administration (NOAA) as a means of providing climate-related science and technical products needed by state and local governments to prepare for the potential impacts of global climate change.

SUPPORT—continued funding for the U.S. Global Climate Change Research Program and the completion of its National Climate Assessment process currently underway under the auspices of the U.S. Global Change Research Act of 1990.

SUPPORT—funding to ensure that the Joint Polar Satellite System (JPSS) is launched as quickly as possible.

SUPPORT—funding for a ''gap-filling'' weather satellite to provide critical data between the end of the current polar satellite's lifetime and the launch of the next-generation Joint Polar Satellite System.

SUPPORT—funding for advanced energy research programs.

Energy and Emissions

SUPPORT—reauthorization of and renewed funding for the Department of Energy's Energy Efficiency and Conservation Block Grant (EECBG) Program.

SUPPORT—continued funding for the U.S. Department of Energy to support the Southeast Florida Clean Cities Coalition and funding for implementation of projects developed under the Clean Cities Community Readiness and Planning for Plug-in Electric Vehicles and Charging Infrastructure, Funding Opportunity Number, DE–FOA–0000451 (Drive Electric Florida & US–1 Corridor Pilot Project).

SUPPORT—continued funding for the U.S. Environmental Protection Agency to support the Southeast Diesel Collaborative and the National Clean Diesel Funding Assistance Program.

Property Assessed Clean Energy (PACE)

SUPPORT—federal legislation that supports local Property Assessed Clean Energy (PACE) programs, specifically by removing barriers to PACE and similar programs for residential properties.

Oil Exploration and Drilling

OPPOSE—oil exploration and drilling in Federal waters on Florida's Outer Continental Shelf.

Everglades Restoration

SUPPORT—the Everglades for the Next Generation Act, which would expedite implementation of projects related to the Comprehensive Everglades Restoration Plan.

SUPPORT—continued focus on Everglades restoration as an essential component of protecting regional water supply and building regional climate resilience.

Tax Policy

SUPPORT—renewal of tax incentives for renewable energy production.

SUPPORT—the elimination of Federal subsidies for oil and gas production.

SUPPORT—renewal of the recently-expired Section 179D of the Internal Revenue Code, which allows deductions for energy efficiency improvements in commercial buildings, and an increase in the per-square-foot value of the deduction from the previous value of $1.80.

SUPPORT—legislation that affirms equal treatment of pretax spending programs for transit and parking and makes future increases in the transit program maximums automatic (as the parking maximum increases already are).

Other

SUPPORT—amending the National Flood Insurance Program (NFIP) to allow multi-peril coverage from a national catastrophic insurance fund.

Climate Change and Sea Level Rise : Adaptation Planning in Broward County, Florida

April 2, 2014

Overview

- Introduction to Broward County
- Climate Change and SLR Impacts
- Planning for Resilience
  - Tools
  - Policy
  - Projects
  - Leadership

Broward County, FL

- Historic Everglades
- 1.8 million residents
- 23 miles of coastline
- Porous geology
- 1,800 miles of canals

Growth in the 21st Century

Interstate 595 Expansion

Fort Lauderdale – Hollywood International Airport Runway Expansion

Port Everglades Channel and Turning Notch Expansion

Vulnerabilities to Climate Change?

Physical characteristics

- Peninsula
- Flat and low lying
- Dense coastal development
- Shallow, transmissive aquifer
- Substantially shaped by water

Climate Change Pressures

- Threats to public and private infrastructure
  - Flooding
  - Beach erosion
  - Severe wind damage
- Strains on water supplies
  - Water shortages
  - Salt water intrusion
- Compromised natural systems
  - Everglades
  - Coral reefs

Winter Storm, Dec. 2010

State Road A1A, Fort Lauderdale, FL
Post Tropical Storm Sandy, Nov. 2012

Hydrology and Sea Level Rise

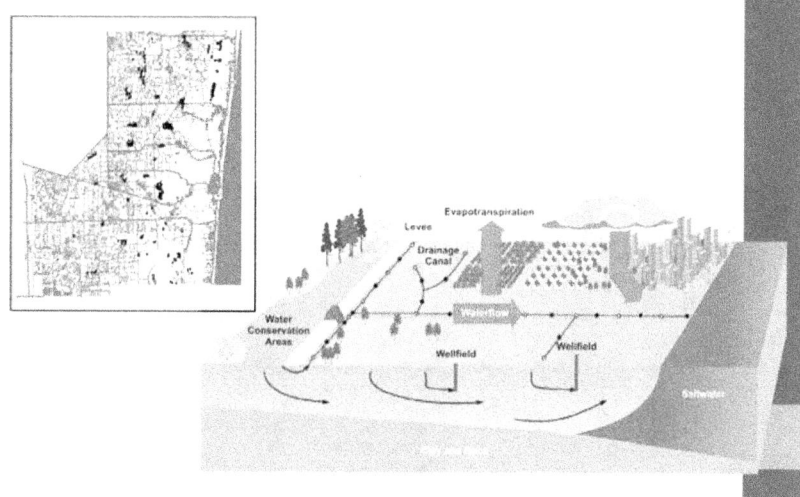

Sea Level Rise and Water Supply

- Saltwater intrusion threatens existing wellfield capacity

- SLR increases this threat

- In Broward County:
  - 2 coastal wellfields are already constrained.
  - 20% (24 MGD) of coastal wellfield capacity is threatened.
  - 60% (70 MGD) of coastal wellfield capacity is considered vulnerable

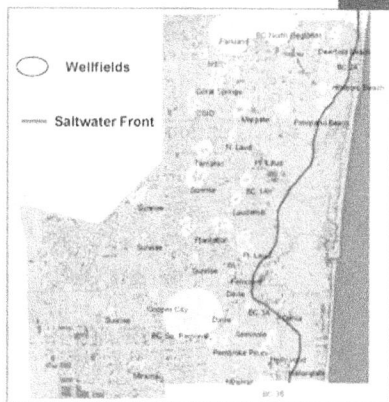

Sea level Rise and Salt Water Intrusion

Combined influences of SLR and pumpage have
accelerated the rate of SW Intrusion 2X rate

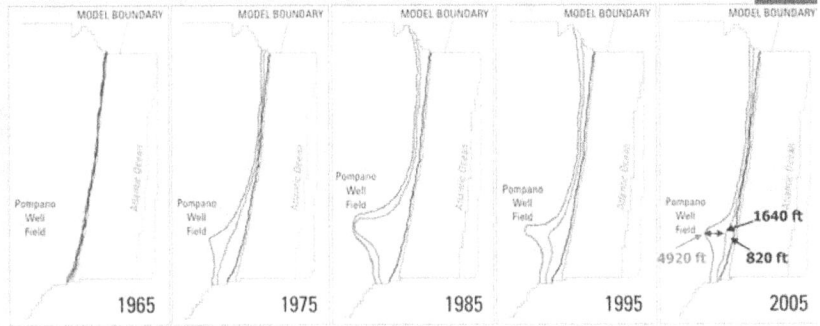

EXPLANATION
Base historical
No sea level
No withdrawals
No sea level rise and no withdrawals

Coastal Flooding
Pre-High Tide Event

High Tide Event

Compromised Drainage Infrastructure

Storm drain located in the cul de sac

Street End with No Waterfront

Inundated street cul de sac, October 2010

Impacts extend to new construction

Coastal impacts translate to inland flooding

Image credit – South Florida Water Management District

Economic Assessment

Taxable Value of Property

	Monroe	Broward	Palm Beach
1 foot	$ 2,763,294,786.00	$ 403,069,831.00	$ 396,618,089.00
2 foot	$ 8,388,138,219.00	$ 1,751,104,870.00	$ 1,251,877,561.00
3 foot	$ 15,087,755,147.00	$ 6,900,509,868.00	$ 3,559,471,158.00

Extreme Weather

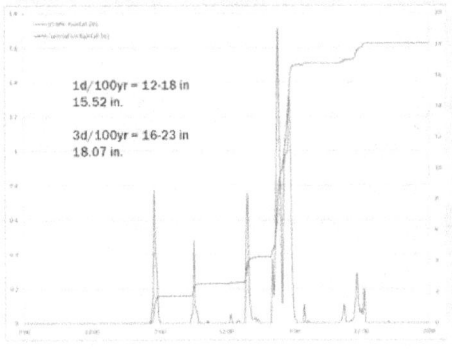

1d/100yr = 12-18 in
15.52 in.

3d/100yr = 16-23 in
18.07 in.

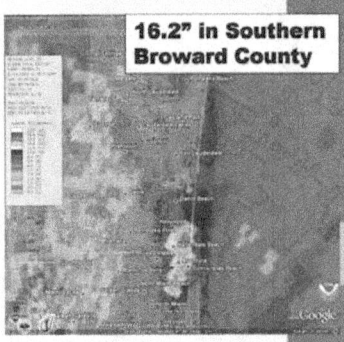

16.2" in Southern Broward County

Severe Weather Erodes Shorelines

Fort Lauderdale, State Road A1A
November 2012
Sandy Impacts compounded by Extreme High Tide

Planning for Sea Level Rise

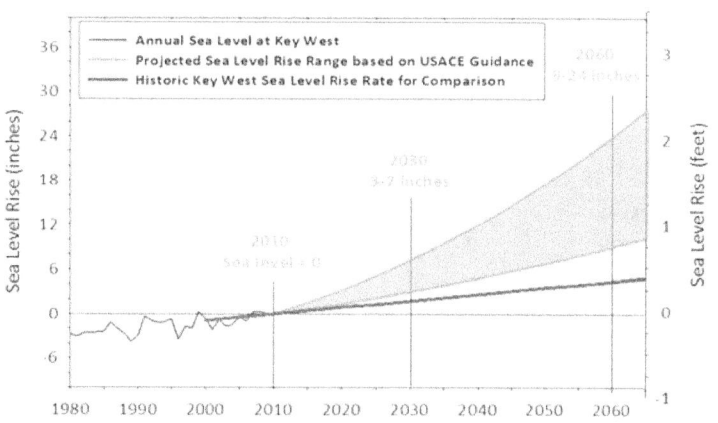

Climate Vulnerability Modeling

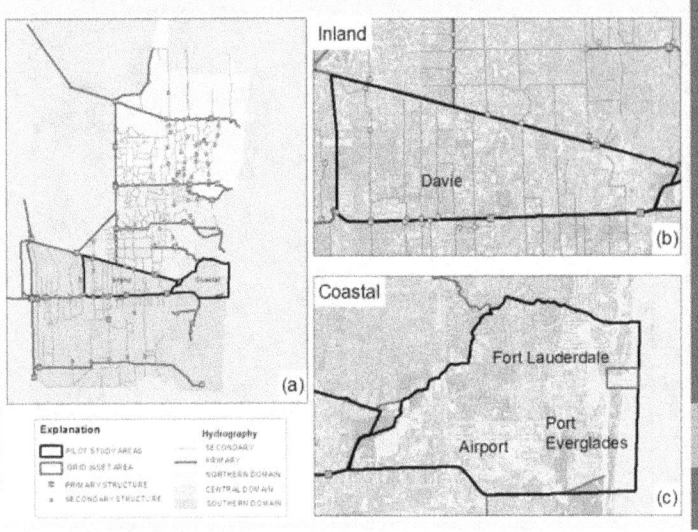

Integrating Aquifer Transmissivity

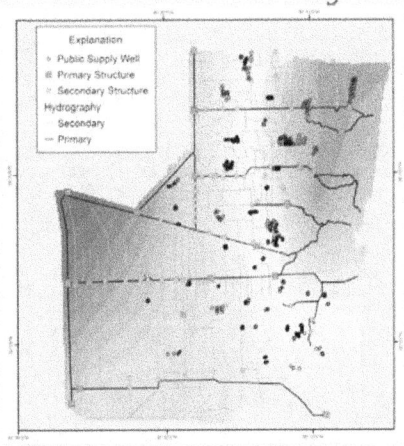

Layering based geological features, Perkins 1977

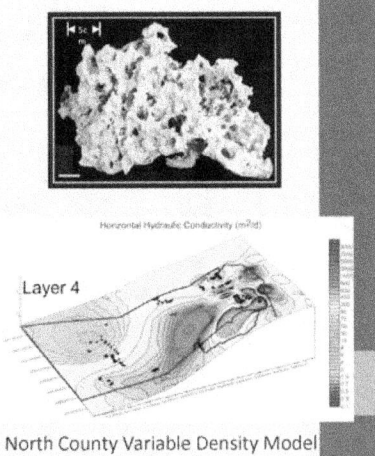

North County Variable Density Model

Inundation Model Details

- Integrated surface/groundwater/variable density models
- Coupled with downscaled climate data from FSU COAPS
- Collaboration with USGS and cost-share provided by Broward County and municipal partners
- Includes
  - GW levels – 2 million records
  - Surface Water – 70 million records
  - 122 surface water control structures
  - 41,860 pumping records
  - Model layers
- Daily and sub daily time steps

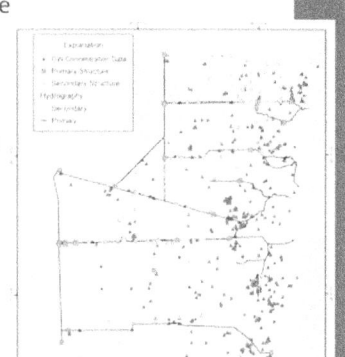

Modeling Scenarios

- High and Low SLR Scenarios
- Design Storm Events
  - 5 year / 1 day
  - 25 year / 3 day
  - 100 year / 3 day
- Extreme High Tide
- Adaptation Strategies

Duration	Return Period (yr)	Broward Rainfall (in)
1 hr	5	3.2
1 day	3	6-6.5
1 day	5	6-8
1 day	10	7-11
1 day	25	9-13
1 day	100	12-18
3 day	10	10-14
3 day	25	12-17
3 day	100	16-23

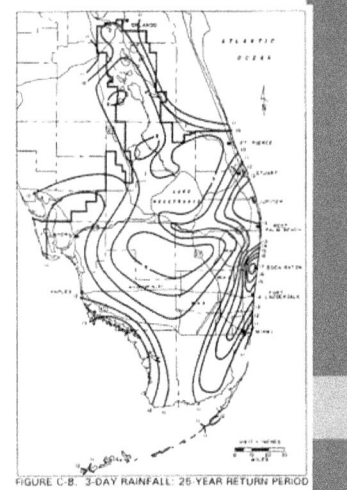

FIGURE C-8. 3-DAY RAINFALL. 25-YEAR RETURN PERIOD

Traditional Model Output

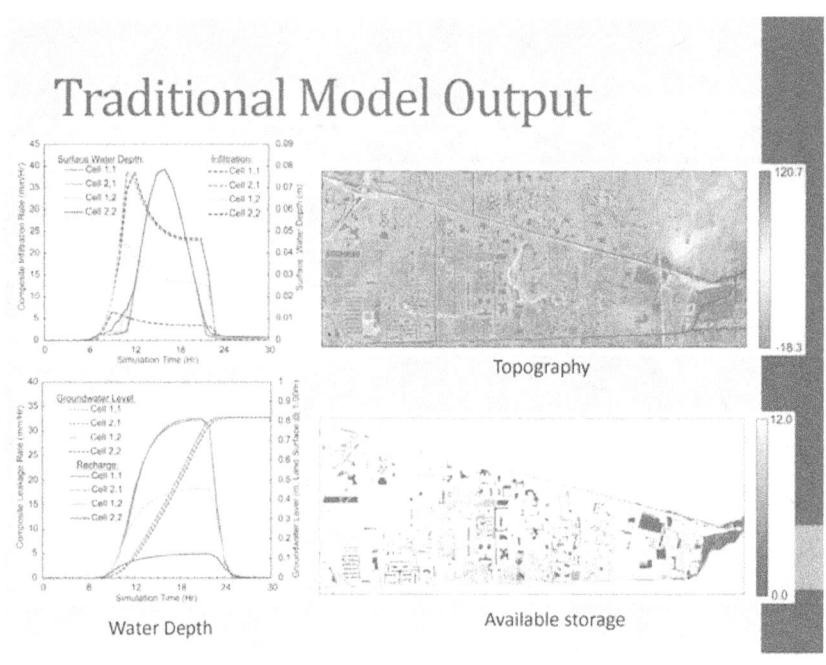

Topography

Water Depth

Available storage

Incorporation of 3D visuals to Better Communicate Risk

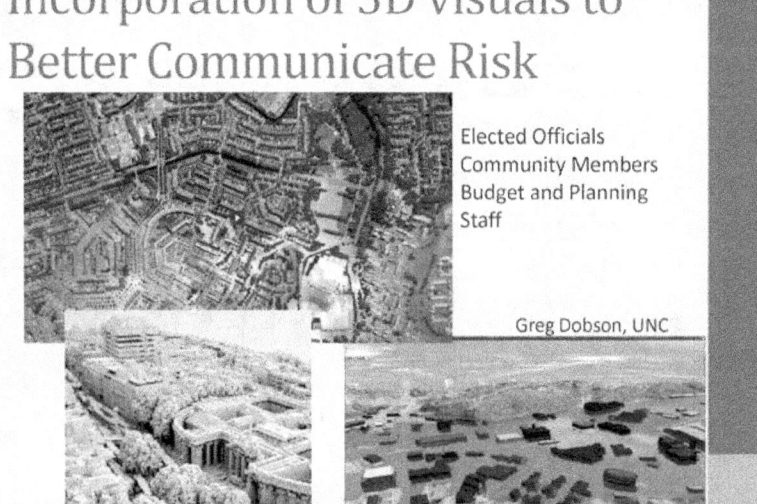

Elected Officials
Community Members
Budget and Planning
Staff

Greg Dobson, UNC

Model Applications for Policy a Planning

- Inform water supply and land use planning
- Update planning and regulatory processes
- Refine Inundation Maps to reflect predicted sea level rise (wet/dry season and design storms)
- Establish new design criteria for:
  - Surface water management systems
  - Transportation planning
  - Building elevations

Lakes Area of Hollywood – 1 Ft Scenario

Leading Climate Resilience

- Adoption of Climate Element as part of County Comprehensive Plan (*National APA Excellence Award)
- Formal integration of sea level rise in county-wide land use plan
- Partners Adaptation - guidance for local governments (Coastal Zone Management Grant)
- Regional resource - providing cities with planning tools, vulnerability maps, climate policies, etc. (Coastal Zone Management Grant)
- Leadership in 4-County Southeast Florida Regional Climate Change Compact

Local and Regional Efforts

- Collaborations to <u>increase awareness</u> about hazards exacerbated by climate change, mitigation, and adaptation strategies.

- Efforts to advance "living shorelines" and green infrastructure as part of <u>regional conservation and management strategies.</u>

- Coordinated <u>restoration of habitat</u> and plans for large-scale connectivity to facilitate habitat shifts.

- Development of <u>communication/decision tools</u> to support infrastructure planning.

Agency Alignment and Action

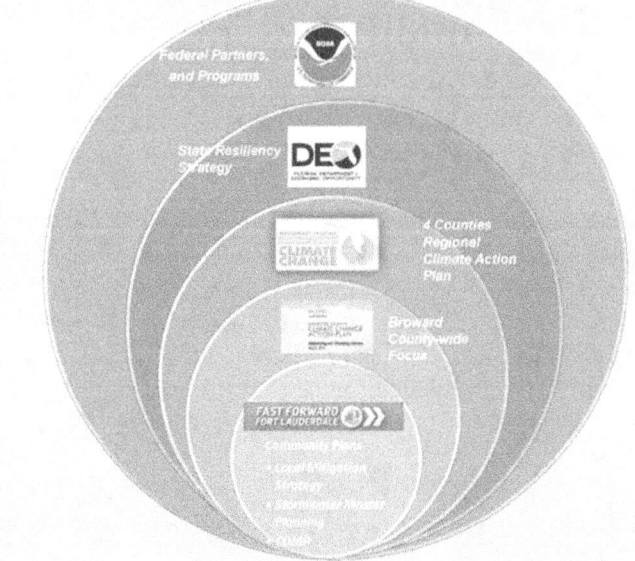

Summary

- Broward County and southeast Florida face significant challenges relating to climate change and sea level rise
- Robust hydrologic models are instrumental to planning activities
- Major capital investments will be needed in advance of realized impacts
- Impacts can be lessened with the integrating of resilient design as part all future projects and planning efforts
- These investments will be fundamental to the health of our communities, protection of the environment, and reducing the risk for severe economic losses.

Commissioner Jacobs also submitted with her prepared statement Southeast Florida Climate Change Regional Compact, ''A Region Responds to a Changing Climate: Southeast Florida Regional Climate Change Compact Counties Regional Climate Action Plan,'' October 12.

The report can be found at *http://www.southeastfloridaclimatecompact.org/wp-content/uploads/2014/09/regional-climate-action-plan-final-ada-compliant.pdf.*

Senator NELSON. Well, Commissioner, I want to thank you. What you all are doing in South Florida, bringing together all these governments, I mean, it sounds like you must be Merlin the Magician to get everybody together and then to support a grant application of one jurisdiction. So thank you, thank you, thank you.

I want you to know that I come to the table not only as someone who has seen Florida grow over the years as a fifth generation Floridian, with my family having come to Florida 185 years ago in 1829, but also because of that experience that Dr. Sellers mentioned. When you look out the window of a spacecraft and look back at our home, it is so beautiful, it is so colorful, it is so alive, it is so creative, and yet it looks so fragile.

If we had a lot of time, Dr. Sellers and I could tell you what you can see from space with the naked eye. Coming across the Amazon region, across Brazil, you could actually see the effects of the destruction of the rainforest because you could see the color contrast. And then you could look to the east, to the mouth of the Amazon, and you could see the siltation, which is natural, but the siltation for hundreds of miles out into the Atlantic because of the destruction of the trees upriver.

On our flight, we could see—I flew a few years before Dr. Sellers—we saw a volcano erupt in Central America, and the westerly winds were carrying the smoke way out into the Pacific. You could see, looking back to the north, the horizon as we came across southern India. You could see the Himalayas looked like they rose to the heavens.

I became more of an environmentalist having had that perspective. And what I concluded from that experience was that I wanted to be a better steward of what the good Lord has given us. And yet, we continue to mess it up.

OK, Dr. Bloetscher, now, you are a scientist right here in our State university system at Florida Atlantic.

Mr. BLOETSCHER. That is right.

Senator NELSON. I want you to share with us what you have concluded.

STATEMENT OF FREDERICK BLOETSCHER, ASSOCIATE PROFESSOR, DEPARTMENT OF CIVIL, ENVIRONMENTAL, AND GEOMATICS ENGINEERING, FLORIDA ATLANTIC UNIVERSITY

Mr. BLOETSCHER. Well, I want to thank you very much, and distinguished guests, for holding this hearing and allowing me to speak at it.

As the other speakers have noted, South Florida is experiencing climate change impacts in primarily sea level rise, but we see a lot of other impacts that are potentially there. But I am going to focus on the sea level rise because it is the one that is permanent. Storms and things like that are temporal in nature.

But we have seen over the last—since 1930, we have seen a steady increase in sea level rise. And keep in mind that most of the drainage system for South Florida was based on 1930s sea level. When we built the drainage systems here over the next 30 years, what we did was we went as far west as we possibly could, drained by gravity. That is why the dikes are out there off of 27, with the assumption that it would drain by gravity to the ocean. Sea level rise kind of frustrates that initial goal, and as a result we see more frequent flooding not only on the coast but inland, because inland doesn't discharge as easily.

We have done some modeling. We have used the NASA satellites, we have used USGS's satellites, we have used NOAA's satellites. And we have come up with some methodologies to convert that to very high-resolution LIDAR, plus or minus six inches, because inches matter in South Florida.

And what we have been able to determine is areas where we are likely to see flooding by matching that up with groundwater levels, which increase as you go west, while typography goes down as you go west. And as a result, we see a lot of area west of I–95, out toward the dike, that we are going to see a lot more frequent flooding. There is less soil capacity, so even smaller rainstorms will cause it to flood.

Those are problems that we are going to have to address as time goes on. Like I said, we have underestimated that.

So what can we do? And the answer, to us, is adaptation. You have already heard from Ms. Jacobs about the counties getting together. Local governments have done some things. Five of the universities in the Florida university system have gotten together. We have created the Florida Climate Institute. FAU is one of the partners, and FAU's focus has been adaptation strategies.

What we look at is, we are able to take apart municipalities, and we have looked specifically at Miami Beach, Miami-Dade County, the Keys, Broward County in some areas, and various other places up into Palm Beach County, and we can identify those areas that are likely vulnerable.

And then we have created some toolboxes of concepts that might work. You are going to see a lot more pumping of stormwater. I think that is an obvious one.

But we are also going to see that some of our coastal salinity structures need to move a lot farther east. If you go up to Dania Beach and Hollywood, the salinity structures are, you know, 10 miles inland. It creates that saltwater intrusion problem that was referenced. We are going to have to change that. There are some in Miami-Dade County that are same way.

Senator NELSON. What is a salinity structure?

Mr. BLOETSCHER. They are basically gates that are put on the canals to keep saltwater from migrating inland, and then it keeps the freshwater behind it. And so the idea is it is a control structure to control the elevation of water.

The problem is, if you put them too far inland, they are actually on the back side of the ridge. And the ridge in South Florida, Henry Flagler, when he built the railroads here, a very smart man, built the railroads on the ridge, the high point, which is about two miles off the coast. If you have a salinity structure that is 10 miles inland, you have a lot of, you know, downslope. And as a result, the water levels back there can't be held as high, and it leads to the saltwater intrusion problem, amongst others.

So we have looked at that. What we see when we start doing this modeling is the roadways are the first things to flood everywhere. And the Mayor has referenced that, and we saw the videos that were going on behind you. You saw a lot of flooding there. And they are the low areas, but it is also where the water and the sewer and the electric and transportation, all the things that we require to live exist in those roadways.

And we are going to see municipalities come up with levels of service, trying to define what is the point at which we are going to try to build to what are the elevations to keep stormwater out.

Now, you have heard a lot of fairly negative news, but I am fairly confident that there are solutions to this problem. We have come up with this toolbox, but there are ideas, there is willingness to do that. There is a lot of planning that is required. It is not an immediate thing; it is a slow, steady creep of sea level rise going up, which allows us to buy some time to do the appropriate planning, not spend money twice for the same thing, build incrementally into those strategies that will help us protect the land that we have and our economy.

I look at the risk issue, and I talk about this a lot. The risk issue is there are 5.7 million people in Southeast Florida, there is almost four trillion dollars' worth of property that is down here, and there is almost $300 billion a year in an economy. That is a significant piece of Florida. It is something that is worth protecting.

So we are going to have to coordinate our efforts. The climate compact was one good way to do that. One government can't do it. You are going to see a lot of local level decisionmaking, but they have to work together, because if one person does it and the other municipality doesn't, it doesn't really help the larger situation.

What is needed? Planning. We are going to have to investigate some technologies that we haven't done, like infiltration trenches to keep road levels low. We have never tried that in Florida. There are some investigations and some testing and research that needs to be done there.

Senator NELSON. What is an infiltration trench?

Mr. BLOETSCHER. It is a concept that is used for water supply in the Midwest. And the idea is that you create a trench and you allow water to flow into it, the groundwater to flow into it, and then you pump it offsite.

They use that in the Midwest along, like, the Ohio River, for example. The Ohio River has a lot of pollutants and things in it. It is very turbid much of the year. And so the idea is they allow the water to flow through the soil into the infiltration trench, and then they pull it off.

We do exfiltration, so we have pipes that are perforated, and water then moves into the soil. The problem is, as sea level rise goes up, the water doesn't go into the soil. But we could repurpose a lot of that if we do some testing and determine how well that would work. And then we could actually pump those things going backward, and it would pull water into those pipes that are perforated.

The idea there being is that along those roadways, especially critical roadways, we could lower the water table along the roadway. It would protect the road base, it would protect the sewers, make the stormwater system work better. But there is an investment in significant dollars that are there.

And in all of the changes that we have here, there is going to be significant dollars and a much more managed system than we have now. But if you look at the value of the economy and the property and what goes on here, there are tools. We do need state, Federal partners to participate.

You know, one of the issues that is there is, so when you do that infiltration trench, where does that water go? It is going to have nutrients in it, things like that, so dumping it into Biscayne Bay or offshore is probably not the right answer. So there is some technology that needs to be investigated. We need to see if we can use some of that water for water supply, but there is some testing to figure out what it is going to take to clean that up.

So we need time. We have some time, but we need to take some steps to start investigating some of these solutions so that when it is time to implement them they are there.

Senator NELSON. Thank you, Professor.

Mr. BLOETSCHER. Thank you very much.

[The prepared statement of Mr. Bloetscher follows:]

53

PREPARED STATEMENT OF FREDERICK BLOETSCHER, ASSOCIATE PROFESSOR, DEPARTMENT OF CIVIL, ENVIRONMENTAL, AND GEOMATICS ENGINEERING, FLORIDA ATLANTIC UNIVERSITY

Senator Nelson and Distinguished Guests,

There has been significant discussion about the potential impacts of climate change on the world: more intense rainfall events, more severe thunderstorms and tropical cyclones, droughts, loss of glacial ice and storage, increased demand for crop irrigation. However for much of the State of Florida, and respectfully for much of the coastal United States east of the Rio Grande River, the climate issue that is most likely to create significant risk to health and economic activity is sea-level rise. Data gathered by NOAA from multiple sites indicates that sea level rise is occurring, and has been for over 100 years (see Figure 1). Similar charts exist across the southeastern U.S. and Gulf states.

The impact of climate change on Florida is two-fold—Florida often is water-supply limited as topography limits the ability to store excess precipitation for water use during the dry periods and sea level rise will exacerbate local flooding. The highly engineered stormwater drainage system of canals and control structures has effectively enabled management of water tables and saltwater intrusion by gravity. The advent of sea-level rise will present new challenges, because the water table is currently maintained at the highest possible levels to counter saltwater intrusion, while limiting flood risk in southeast Florida's low-lying terrain and providing for water supplies. As sea level rises, the water will not flow by gravity, which disrupts that balance struck between flood risk and water supply availability in the canal system.

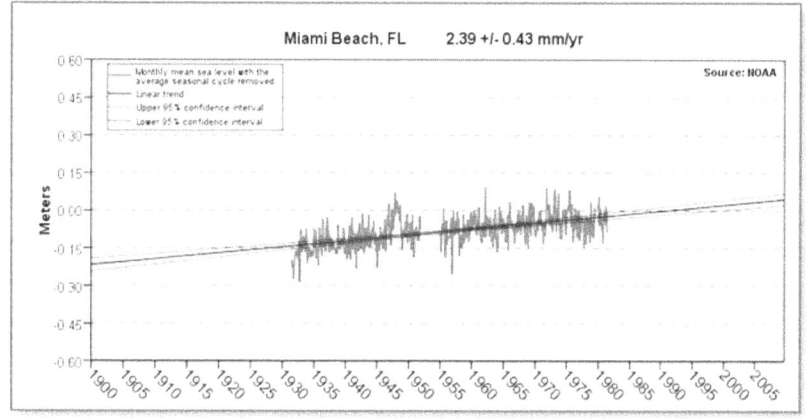

Figure 1. Sea Level Rise in Miami Beach, 1930–1980

Occasional flooding is not new to Florida, but the increasing frequency we currently experience is related to sea level rise, not just along the coast, but for large expanses of developed property inland due to topography and groundwater levels. As a result, the challenge for water managers in the state, especially in southeast Florida, is to control the groundwater table, because control of the water table is essential to prevent flooding of the low terrain.

The issue is not lost on local governments in south Florida nor on the educational institutions in the area. Florida Universities are playing in helping this region and the State to both understand the State of the art in the science of sea level rise and other climate related changes and to identify ways in which we can mitigate, respond to and adapt to these changes. My university, Florida Atlantic University, is located in this vulnerable part of the State has been proactive in partnership with the Four County Compact in addressing these issues and we have now joined with FIU and five other Universities in the State to form the Florida Climate Institute, a consortium working with state and Federal agencies to address the multiple challenges and opportunities facing this State. FAU has been proactive in developing tools to evaluate risk and identify adaptation strategies to protect local and regional infrastructure and property.

I illustrate this approach by looking at our recent study of the Impact of Sea level Rise on Urban Infrastructure which I have submitted as a separate document. Our efforts have included using high resolution NOAA data to map topography at the +/-6 inch level, combined that topography with mapping of infrastructure and groundwater, to identify vulnerable areas throughout Broward, Miami-Dade and Monroe Counties, as well as initiated projects in Palm Beach County and other coastal regions throughout the state. By identifying vulnerability based on sea level changes, the timing and tools for adaptation can be designed and funded to insure a ''no-regrets'' strategy that neither accelerates nor delays infrastructure beyond its need.

We have all heard the discussion an addition rise in sea level of an estimated two to three feet is anticipated by 2100; some scientists think it will be more. But sea level rise is a slow, albeit permanent change to our environment. The slow part allows us to make informed decisions about adaptation strategies that may prove useful in the long term as well as the short term. Of prime importance is the need to plan for these needs 50 or more years out so that we do not increase our exposure to risk. Keeping development out of low lying areas, redeveloping pumping and piping systems with change in mind and reserving areas where major efforts will need to be undertaken, is important to the public interest and will affect private business, tourism and homeowners. Sea level rise is already a problem for many low lying areas such as Miami Beach, Fort Lauderdale, Hollywood, and other coastal communities. It will be an incremental problem creeping up on us for the rest of the century and beyond.

In Miami Beach, as elsewhere in Florida, the lowest lying areas are the roadways, which are also the location of electrical, water, sewer, phone and drainage infrastructure. Fortunately given the current Federally funded special imagery and NOAA data systems we are able to predict pretty accurately where flooding will occur. Linking that information with our detailed projections of sea level rise impacts we can begin now to map vulnerability and build adaptive measures into every action and plan we undertake. Figure 2 shows the issue with current, 1, 2 and 3 feet of sea level rise. Looking at a particularly vulnerable area, Miami Beach, it is clear that the percentage of land that will be impacted on a daily basis will increase with time as sea level rises (see Figure 3).

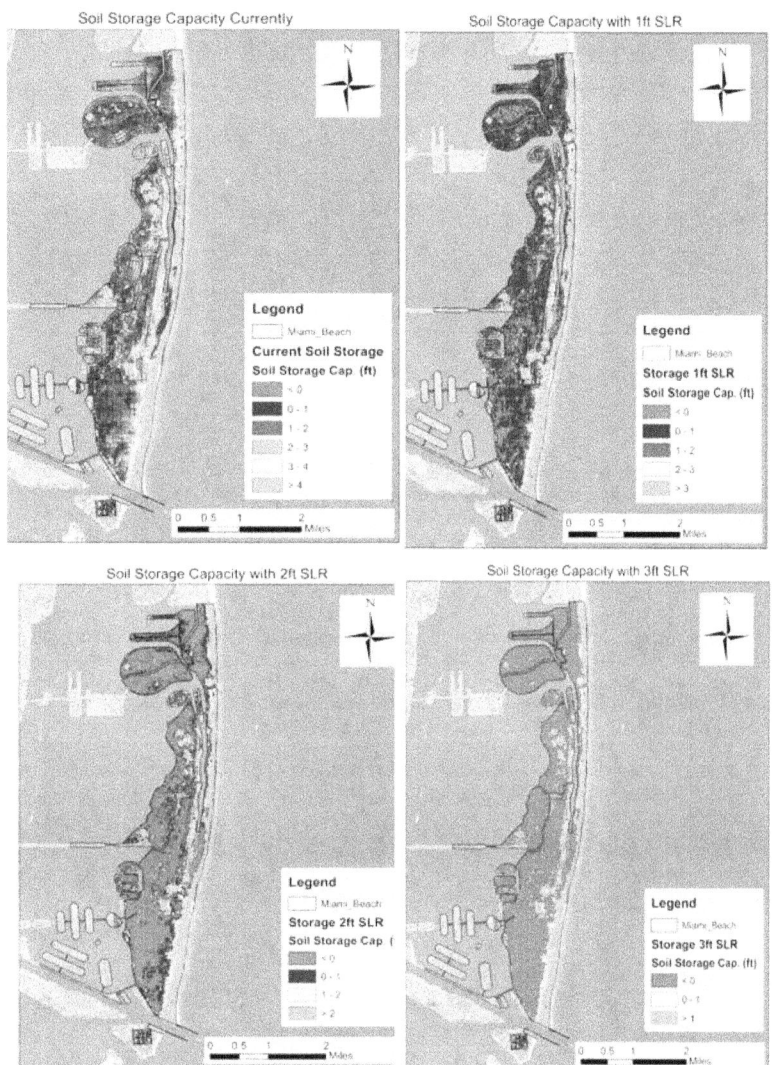

Figure 2. Rise of Sea Level in Miamia Beach, 0, 1, 2, 3 ft

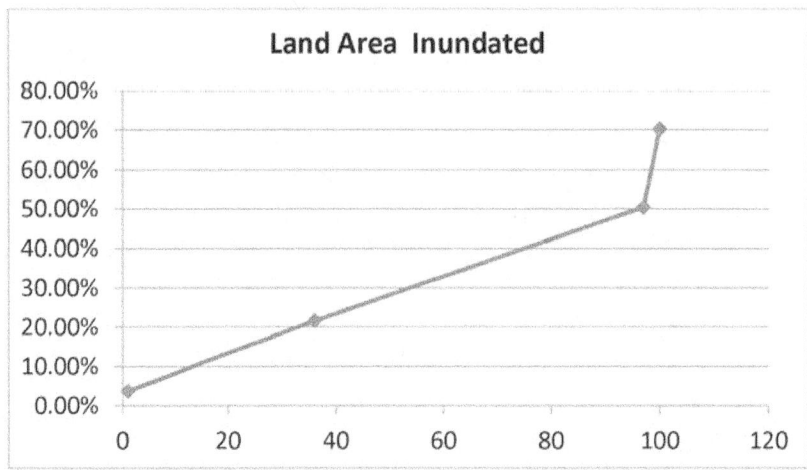

Figure 3. Increase in percent of properties that will flood during high tides at some point during the day as Sea Level Rises in Miami Beach

But the impacts are not only on the coast. Sea level affects ground water table levels and with our intense rainfall areas far inland can be flooded, even subject to long term inundation. Water levels are rising and will continue to rise as groundwater rises concurrently with sea level. Add the impact summer rains and dealing with water becomes a major priority. Figures 4 and 5 outline the roadway network degradation at present, 1, 2, and 3 ft of sea level rise. The figures demonstrate that a major, underestimated amount of property is vulnerable on the western edge of the developed areas because the elevations are decreasing as one moves west from I95.

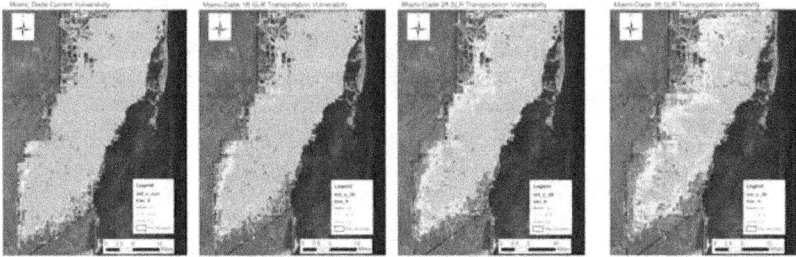

Figure 4. Miami-Dade County for groundwater-adjusted model results.

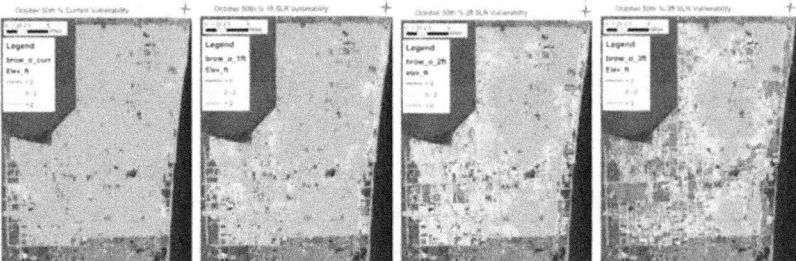

Figure 5. Broward County for groundwater-adjusted model results.

While time will impact our environment, we have three options to address the change:

• Protect infrastructure from the impacts of climate change

- Adapt to the changes, and
- In the worst case retreat from the change.

We do not believe retreat needs to be considered n the short or medium term. South Florida has developed in the last 100 years and we think there will be well over 100 years of life left. As a result, our best option is adaptation. Adaptation takes different forms depending on location. For example we can install more coastal salinity structures, raise road beds, abandon some local roads, increase storm water pumping, add storm water retention etc. to address many of the problems. The technology is available today.

FAU has developed a toolbox of options that can be applied to address these adaptation demands, resulting in an approach that will need a more managed integrated water system, more operations and inevitably more dollars. Much of the actual needs are local, but the problem is regional and requires a concerted effort of federal, state and local agencies and the private sector to address the scales of the problem. A community can address the local problems, but the regional canals, barriers, etc., are beyond the scope of individual agencies. Collaboration and discussion are needed. The Four County Compact is an excellent example, but the longer term solutions need the state and Federal agencies and the related dollars to address larger impacts.

The needs will be large—in the tens of billions. But there are two things in south Florida's favor—time and money. The expenditures are over many, many years. Most important in the near term need is the early planning and identification of critical components of infrastructure and policy needs and timing for same. That is what FAU does best. At risk are nearly 6 million of Floridians their economy and lifestyle, $3.7 trillion in property (2012) in south east Florida alone and a $260 billion annual economy. All of these are expected to continue to increase assuming the appropriate plans are made to adapt to the changing sea level. Protection of the area for the next 100–150 years is achievable as long as we have the science, the understanding and the will to do it. Plan now, and over the rest of this century starting now we can raise those billions of dollars needed.

Senator NELSON. All right. Mr. Talbert?

STATEMENT OF WILLIAM D. TALBERT III, PRESIDENT AND CHIEF EXECUTIVE OFFICER, GREATER MIAMI CONVENTION & VISITORS BUREAU

Mr. TALBERT. Thank you very much, Senator. Bill Talbert, President and CEO of the Greater Miami Convention and Visitors Bureau, the official destination sales and marketing company for greater Miami and Miami Beach.

I would like to ask that you not have me follow Mayor Levine next time. He is way too good at what he does. I would like to maybe go first, if I could.

[Laughter.]

Mr. TALBERT. And we are a partner, we have a relationship with the City of Miami Beach.

And I want you to know, Senator, that I, too, like you, was born in the state of Florida. My mother served in the Navy in Jacksonville during World War II, and I grew up there. And I can tell you that living in Jacksonville Beach, we spent most of our time in the water, in the surf. Early surfers in Jacksonville. I then was honored to graduate from Florida Atlantic in Boca with a master's degree. They were very tolerant there, so——

[Laughter.]

Mr. BLOETSCHER. Glad to have you.

Mr. TALBERT. Thank you.

And I have been in this community for 40 years-plus.

Let me just talk about the numbers. And I am going to give you numbers, targeted numbers.

Travel and tourism is greater Miami and the beaches' number one industry. For the past four years, greater Miami and Miami Beach has experienced record numbers of visitors. In 2013, a record 14.2 million visitors spent one or more nights in greater Miami and Miami Beach and spent a record $22.8 billion in this community.

In 2013, for the first time in our history, greater Miami was visited by more international visitors than domestic. For the past four years and three months, the hospitality sector in greater Miami and Miami Beach has added jobs each month—each month—a record 114,700 jobs. Seventy-five percent of all of those 14.2 million visitors came for a vacation—vacation. Greater Miami is blessed with approximately 25 miles of world-class beaches.

The Greater Miami Convention and Visitors Bureau collects information from independent third parties—collected by independent third parties. Approximately 400 interviews are conducted each month. Our surveys in 2013 showed the following.

Forty-five percent of all of our visitors stayed here on Miami Beach, largely in hotels—largely in hotels. We asked them, what do you like? Now, they have multiple likes. Fifty-six percent said their most-liked feature was the weather. Forty-two percent said their most-liked feature was right where we are here, South Beach and Ocean Drive.

Right, Mary? You like that?

[Laughter.]

Mr. TALBERT. Thirty-nine, almost 40 percent said their most-liked feature was the beaches. And then 32 percent said sunbathing.

During the recent BP oil spill, we learned the importance of the global perception of the condition of our beaches. While no oil from the BP oil spill made it to greater Miami or Miami Beach's beaches, the perception of, "oil on Florida's beaches" had the potential to negatively affect tourism to greater Miami. In fact, because of this potential, BP provided us a grant to kind of tell the world that there was no oil on our beaches. Remember, 25 miles of beaches. Why are they coming for a vacation and beaches a large part of that.

Greater Miami travel and tourism continues to prosper. Greater Miami and Miami Beach have evolved to be a great global community. Greater Miami and Miami Beach is now one of the top tourist destinations in the world. Great weather, great access, international ambiance, heritage neighborhoods, thriving in arts and culture, world-class shopping, world-class dining, and, of course, pristine beaches.

We are looking, as a private destination sales and marketing company for countywide, Miami Beach, a good—a leader as a partner, is to work with the governments, both the City of Miami Beach under its new leadership and the County of Dade. Harvey Ruvin and I have worked together for a long time. And those government partners, we are working directly with them on these serious issues.

And we commend you, Senator, for your leadership on this issue. These are serious issues.

Thank you.

[The prepared statement of Mr. Talbert follows:]

PREPARED STATEMENT OF WILLIAM D. TALBERT III, PRESIDENT AND CHIEF
EXECUTIVE OFFICER, GREATER MIAMI CONVENTION & VISITORS BUREAU

Travel and Tourism is Greater Miami's #1 Industry

For the past four years Greater Miami has experienced record numbers of visitors.
In 2013, a record 14.2 million visitors spent one or more nights in Greater Miami
and spent a record $22.8 billion dollars in our community.

In 2013, for the first time in our history, Greater Miami was visited by more
international visitors than domestic. For the past 4 years and 3 months the hospitality sector in Greater Miami has added jobs each month . . . a record 114,700
jobs. 75 percent plus of Greater Miami's Overnight Visitors come to the community
for a "vacation."

Greater Miami is blessed with approximately 25 miles of world class beaches. The
Greater Miami Convention and Visitors Bureau [GMCVB] collects this information
from independent third parties. Approximately 400 interviews of visitors are conducted each month by GMCVB independent contractors. The GMCVB's most recent
surveys show the following:

- 45 percent of the Overnight Visitors stayed on Miami Beach
- 56 percent of Overnight Visitors said their "Most Liked Feature(s)" of Greater
  Miami was: Weather (multiple answers permitted)
- 42 percent said: South Beach/Ocean Drive
- 39 percent said: Beaches
- 32 percent said: Sun Bathing

During the recent BP Oil Spill we learned the importance of the global perception
of the condition of our beaches. While no oil from the BP Oil Spill made it to Greater Miami's beaches the perception of 'oil on Florida's beaches had the potential to
negatively affect tourism to Greater Miami. In fact, because of this potential, BP
provided grant assistance to the GMCVB to deal with this issue. Largely because
no oil made it to Miami's beaches, there was no negative impact from the BP Oil
Spill.

Greater Miami travel and tourism continues to prosper. Greater Miami has
evolved to become a great global community. Greater Miami is now one of the top
tourist destinations in the world. Great weather, great access, international ambiance, heritage neighborhood, thriving arts and culture, world class shopping, world
class dining and, of course, pristine beaches.

[Applause.]

Senator NELSON. So could you sum up your testimony by saying,
"No beaches, no bucks"?

Mr. TALBERT. That is correct.

Senator NELSON. Dr. Linkin, thank you——

Mr. TALBERT. And no jobs.

Senator NELSON. Indeed.

Dr. Linkin, I am especially pleased to have you. Your industry
at large, not your specific reinsurance industry, but your industry
at large is the grease that allows all of these businesses and resi-
dences to continue, because you insure them.

And Swiss Re, a reinsurance company, reinsures against catastrophe. So we have a coming catastrophe. Tell us what the insurance industry is doing about it.

**STATEMENT OF MEGAN LINKIN, NATURAL HAZARDS EXPERT,
SWISS RE**

Ms. LINKIN. OK. Thank you, Senator Nelson and to the City of
Miami Beach, for hosting me today.

My name is Megan Linkin, and, as the Senator said, I am a Natural Hazards Expert for Swiss Re.

Now, like you, sir, and like Mr. Talbert, I actually grew up in a
coastal community, as well. I grew up in the North on the New Jer-
sey shore, but it was the love of that community and the beach

60

that made me enter a career where I could look at addressing climate change.

Swiss Re, we are a global reinsurer. We are headquartered in Zurich, Switzerland. Last year, we marked our 150th anniversary, and one of the cornerstones of us marking our 150th anniversary was the very loud message that climate change is happening. It is going to increase risk throughout the world, especially to those cities and population centers that are located on the coast.

Climate change, as many others have mentioned here already this morning, is expected to alter the frequency and severity of many extreme weather events, from tropical cyclones to floods to droughts and to extreme rainfall events.

And even currently, without climate change, we are vulnerable to extreme weather events due to the globalization of the economy and our increasing reliance on technology. We saw this vulnerability during Hurricane Sandy in 2012, the September 2013 floods in Colorado, and the extreme winter that the Northeast and the Central Plains experienced just this past year.

And while we don't know whether these individual weather events are attributable to climate change or natural variations in the climate system, known as climate variability, we do know that these events are in line with the expected impacts of climate change in the coming decades.

It is impossible to attribute any of the insured and economic weather-related loss to climate change. We simply at this point in time don't have the means to separate the two influencers. But what we do know is this: The risk posed by coastal flood is indisputably growing due to rising sea levels.

And this is going to pose a risk to many of our coastal communities, and the potential loss in terms of property and lives is tremendous. We should never lose sight of the fact that over 1,800 people perished during Hurricane Katrina because of the storm surge and inadequate preventative measures that were put in place.

Many coastal communities are exposed to sea level rise and flood, but few more so than the communities which are located in the United States. Coastal and shoreline communities in the U.S. account for approximately $6.6 trillion of the United States GDP and about 51 million jobs.

And the risk to coastal communities is going to be not only driven by sea level rise but also by the increasing population and assets situated in these high-risk areas. As Mr. Talbert noted, the weather here is really nice.

[Laughter.]

Ms. LINKIN. And if the current population trends continue, the U.S. coastal population is projected to grow from 123 million people to nearly 135 million people by 2020.

Florida provides a good example, as you already mentioned, of the risk posed to the U.S. coastline by sea level rise, with approximately 8,500 miles of tidal shoreline and over 75 percent of the state's population residing in coastal counties. And the inevitable cost to recover from these coastal and inland flood events, especially in major cities, in Miami, are going to be significant and much greater than anything we have ever experienced before.

Coastal communities thrive on their proximity to the coast and the development of these regions, which create jobs, revenue, and enhances the prosperity of the community. However, there are perverse incentives at play because of the enormous economic incentive to develop high-risk coastal areas, which then puts further people and assets at risk.

And as we have already seen many times, the costs when disaster strikes are externalized. The Federal Government and then inevitably the taxpayers are expected to foot the bill. We must rethink this approach in order to reduce risk and protect our communities.

And, therefore, we must take action today to prepare ourselves for the climate of tomorrow. This means controlling and mitigating our risk to sea level rise through a variety of measures, including building and zoning codes, seawalls, reinforcing or relocating key infrastructure, building elevation, and other measures.

It also means integrating climate risk considerations into our planning process. For example, if we expect a building or a piece of infrastructure to have a lifespan of 60 years, then it must be built not only to withstand the climate today but the likely climate in the next 60 years.

Until we start to integrate climate change into these processes— for example, including sea level risk projections into FEMA flood maps—we will constantly be creating more problems for future generations to take care of and potentially creating an ever-growing portfolio of stranded assets.

Insurance is a key component of any holistic risk management strategy. Insurance cannot replace what is irreplaceable, such as land and lives, but it can provide both persons and governments with the financial means to recover and rebuild quickly.

The insurance industry and the reinsurance industry are resilient, innovative, and experts in risk evaluation. Throughout the years, we have worked alongside the government in implementing standards that have reduced economic loss, saved lives, and educated the consumer to the true risk faced by them. An example of that already is seatbelts that are now standard in all motor vehicles.

Typically, to generate the underwriting and actuarial tools that we use to assess risk posed by natural catastrophes, we rely on data from the U.S. Government. And this includes information from all sources: the USGS, NOAA, the Storm Prediction Center, the Hurricane Research Division, and any other official sources. Once any information is published by these official sources, we can incorporate this into our model. And this includes sea level rise changes.

Presently, I know of no insurance or reinsurance company that directly includes the risk of climate change in their model. And that is because our product is typically contracted on an annual basis, and in that time period the impact of any climate changes, including sea level rise, are too small and insignificant and without scientific consensus to responsibly include in our modeling approach.

Senator NELSON. But you wouldn't say that over the last couple of decades, would you? Would not the fact of sea level rise be some part of the calculation of what the insurance premium was going to be?

Ms. LINKIN. Correct. And that is why it is so critical that we continue to get this reliable and official information from these government sources, such as NASA. Because, although we don't include it explicitly, we do so every time we update the models and the actuarial tools and the pricing tools, because we update them with the most up-to-date scientific information, the most up-to-date hazard information, and the most up-to-date state of the climate so that when we are assessing risk we are assessing risk under the climate conditions that we see today, not the climate conditions that we saw 50 years ago.

Senator NELSON. So these policies that look only one to three years in the future, is that the reason that the insurance industry really hasn't come to the table as a partner in this climate change concern?

Ms. LINKIN. Actually, from the perspective of a reinsurer, I believe that we have. We have developed a methodology that allows us to incorporate climate change information within our models and come up with economic loss projections under today's climate and under future climate-change scenarios. We refer to this methodology as the economics of climate adaptation, and it has been successfully deployed globally.

And one of the areas that it was successfully deployed in was South Florida, which, for our definition, was Broward County, Miami-Dade County, and Palm Beach. And what we showed is that, in spite of a potential annual cost of tropical cyclones impacting approximately 10 percent of the local GDP, by 2030 over 40 percent of the total expected loss could be averted using cost-effective measures, such as beach renourishment and vegetation management.

So we very much acknowledge that this is an issue, and we very much want to help our partners, whether or not they are Federal Governments, State governments, municipal governments, county governments, or primary insurers, understand what their risks are today and what kind of risk they will be facing in the future.

Senator NELSON. So you are saying that you do build in an incentive for people to start looking at climate change, by virtue of what you just said. Is that correct?

Ms. LINKIN. If we are contracted and sanctioned by somebody to do so, we can demonstrate to them what sort of resiliency measures would be beneficial for them to put in place to offset many of their losses that they might experience under a changed climate.

Senator NELSON. If they contact you.

Ms. LINKIN. Yes.

Senator NELSON. What are you doing proactively, if anything, to incentivize folks to get prepared for what is going to occur?

Ms. LINKIN. We do it through a lot of outreach. We do it through a lot of education. We engage very often with governments to make sure that they understand their risk. We have deployed tools that our clients have access to, which allow them to assess their risk through just simple mapping routines.

So we really help our clients focus on what their risk is today, and if they ask, we are more than happy to help them focus on what their risks are in the future.

Senator NELSON. The position of a reinsurance company is to insure and spread the risk of catastrophe. The reinsurance industry has been critical to Florida in spreading the risk of huge loss with regard to hurricanes.

Does the insurance industry think as a result of climate change that we are going to see greater frequency and more ferocity of storms as a result of the rising temperature?

Ms. LINKIN. Yes, we agree with the assessments that were put forth by the IPCC in the most recent report.

Senator NELSON. So, ergo, does that mean that the cost of insuring against wind damage becomes greater?

Ms. LINKIN. In the future, once we start to see the influence and once it is discernable within the hazard, we are going to see that have an impact on insurance premiums. If we see the current hazard and risk landscape change and the cost of losses goes up, then, by definition, the cost of insuring that risk will go up.

Senator NELSON. And you mentioned Hurricane Katrina, that it was an event that the real damage was not a Category 3 wind, it was the fact that in the counterclockwise winds they raised the level of Lake Pontchartrain, it raised the level of the water in the canals, the pressure built and breached the canals and filled up the bowl of New Orleans.

Now, if the sea levels rise, what does the experience of Katrina tell us for a lot of our infrastructure from the insurance companies? standpoint?

Ms. LINKIN. It is going to demonstrate that that infrastructure is going to be very vulnerable to damage. There could be some assets that become uninsurable, not because we are not able to offer insurance—the industry has plenty of capacity—but because the premium rates might become high, which would lead to consumers not wanting to pay.

Senator NELSON. I think you have summed it up right there.

[The prepared statement of Ms. Linkin follows:]

PREPARED STATEMENT OF MEGAN LINKIN, NATURAL HAZARDS EXPERT, SWISS RE

Chairman Rockefeller, Ranking Member Thune, Senator Nelson, and other members of the Committee on Commerce, Science, and Transportation my name is Megan Linkin and I'm a Natural Hazards Expert for Swiss Re. Swiss Re is a global reinsurance company and last year marked our 150th anniversary. I thank you for the opportunity to testify in front of the Committee regarding the implications of sea level rise and climate change. Swiss Re recognizes that climate change will increase risk throughout the world, especially to those cities and population centers situated along the coast.

Climate change is expected to alter the frequency and severity of many extreme weather events, such as floods, droughts and rainfall. Even currently, we are vulnerable to extreme weather events, due to the globalization of the economy and increasing reliance on technology. We witnessed our vulnerability during Hurricane Sandy, the September 2013 floods in Colorado and the extreme winter of 2013/14.

At present, it is difficult to determine whether or not these recent, extreme meteorological events are attributable to climate change or climate variability. Regardless, these events are in line with the expected impacts of climate change in the coming decades. It is impossible to attribute any of the insured or economic weather related loss to climate change—we simply don't have the means currently to discern how much, if any, of the loss was caused by climate change.

What we do know is this: The risk posed by coastal flood is indisputably growing, due to rising sea levels. The increasing risk that it poses to many of our coastal communities will be tremendous in terms of loss of property and potentially a loss in life. We should never lose sight of the fact that over 1,800 people perished due to the storm surge and inadequate preventative measures in place prior to Hurricane Katrina.

Many countries are highly exposed to sea level rise and flood, few more so than the United States. Coastal and shoreline communities account for approximately $6.6 trillion to U.S. GDP,[1] and 51 million[2] jobs. The risk to coastal communities is not only driven by sea level rise, but increasing population and assets situated in these high risk areas. If current population growth trends continue, the U.S. coastal population will grow from 123 million people to nearly 134 million people by 2020.[3]

Florida provides a good example of the risk posed to the U.S. coastline, with over 8,400 miles of tidal shoreline and over 75 percent of the state's population residing in coastal counties. The inevitable costs to recover from these events, especially in major cities like Miami, are going to be significant and much greater than anything that we have ever experienced before.

Coastal communities thrive on their proximity to the coast and the development of these regions. Coastal development creates jobs, revenue, and enhances the prosperity of the community. However, there are perverse incentives at play because of the enormous economic incentive to develop high risk coastal areas, which then puts further people and assets at risk. As we have seen many times, the costs when disaster strikes are externalized; the Federal Government and the taxpayers are expected to foot the bill. We must rethink this approach in order to reduce the risk and protect our communities.

Therefore, we must act today to prepare for tomorrow. This means controlling and mitigating our risk to sea level rise through a variety of measures including building and zoning codes, sea walls, reinforcing or relocating key infrastructures, building elevations and other measures.

It also means integrating climate risk considerations into our planning processes. For example, if we expect a building to have a life span of 60 years then it must to be built to withstand the likely climate of 60 years in the future. Until we start to integrate climate change into these processes we will be constantly creating more problems for future generations to take care of and potentially creating an ever growing portfolio of "stranded assets". A simple example is incorporating sea level risk projections into FEMA flood maps.

Insurance is a key component of any holistic risk management strategy. Insurance cannot replace what is irreplaceable, such as land and lives, but it can provide both persons and governments with the financial means to recover and rebuild quickly. The insurance industry is resilient, innovative, and experts in risk evaluation. Throughout the years we have worked alongside the government in implementing standards that have reduced economic loss, saved lives and educating the consumer to the true risks faced by them.

Typically the hazard component of all natural catastrophe models is based on data published by the United States Government. This would include current information provided by the United States Geological Survey, National Ocean and Atmospheric Administration, the National Weather Service's Storm Prediction Center, the Hurricane Research Center and other official sources. Once any information published by these official sources is published, including sea level changes, we incorporate these changes within our models.

Presently I know of no insurance company or reinsurer that directly includes the risk of climate change into their models. Our product, insurance, is typically contracted on an annual basis. Within that time period the impact of any climate changes including sea level rise are too insignificant and without scientific consensus to responsibly include in our modeling approach.

Although we do not directly include climate change within our models we may unknowingly be doing so within each catastrophe model update that we do. Every couple of years our models are updated to reflect the loss history and the scientific findings after the most recent events. As such any influence that climate change has on these events is implicitly included. Even though there is not direct/explicit loading for climate change in our models, we take the issue very seriously and conduct research which does specifically take climate change factors into consideration.

---

[1] Source: NOAA

[2] Source BLS

[3] Source: NOAA

The insurance industry, particularly Swiss Re, has pioneered studies which investigate the economic loss potential from extreme weather events, and savings from the implementation of various resiliency measures, in the present and in a new climate regime caused by climate change. This methodology, which we refer to as the ''Economics of Climate Adaptation,'' has been successfully deployed globally. South Florida (Broward, Miami-Dade and Palm Beach) is one of the locations where the analysis was performed; the results showed that in spite of a potential annual cost of tropical cyclones impacts costing the equivalent of 10 percent of local GDP by 2030, over 40 percent of the total expected loss could be averted using cost effective measures such as beach nourishment and vegetation management.[4]

If we fail to act we will be faced with the astronomical cost to recover from our inaction and we may also see the availability of insurance becoming scare at an affordable price. We will always have the capacity to insure and reinsure but the impact of a steady gradual increase in frequency and severity because of these higher risks could lead to higher premiums, which many consumers may not want to pay. Without insurance, communities will be slower to recover and many may not recover at all.

We recognize that Florida has been at the forefront of tacking action to deal with severe weather impacts no more so in places like Broward County. In Broward County officials have recognized the increased risk and are acting upon it. We urge the rest of Florida to act now in a unified fashion. We support the actions taken by his committee and thank you again for asking Swiss Re to testify. I look forward to answering any follow-up questions from the Committee.

Senator NELSON. OK. Do any of the panelists have a question for another one of the panelists?

Ms. LINKIN. I have a question, Senator, for either the Mayor or the Commissioner.

In your risk management strategies and adaptation strategies to climate change and sea level rise, are you considering looking at insurance products to help protect against residual risks?

Because no matter how much you improve pumping systems, seawalls, any sort of infrastructure, there is always going to be that residual risk component remaining. Is insurance an option for financially protecting against that risk?

Ms. JACOBS. I think one of the important things that Broward County is doing, and, in fact, we were able to get it into State law and we have been trying to have it adopted on the Federal side, and that is what we call adaptation action areas, through LIDAR technology, to understand where our vulnerabilities are.

So when we start looking at increased costs of insurance, when we look at the dollars that we have or that we are asking for from other funders, whether it is the State or the Federal Government, that we are putting those dollars into making those areas more resilient, including in this language in our land development code, so all new projects that get built will have to consider climate change into the future based on the modeling that the four counties have done. That, in turn, affects what we are going to be paying for our insurance.

So understanding where those vulnerabilities are I think is the first step. And understanding how to then prioritize around those vulnerabilities to spend our dollars wisely will help us stand up to or be more prepared for dealing with increased insurance costs.

There is a lot of discussion about retreat, when do you start having to tell people, ''No, don't live in that area.'' And I have always said that the insurance is going to help push that decision forward.

---

[4] Source: Economics of Climate Adaptation main report: *http://media.swissre.com/documents/rethinking\shaping\climate\resilent\development\en.pdf*

We are not going to have to, I believe, as government, go out and say, ''This area has been redlined. We are no longer going to address roadway problems or drainage problems. We are going to go focus somewhere else.'' I don't think we are going to find ourselves in that position. Rather, I think we are going to find people choosing to live and move somewhere else.

And a recent example would be a business on Las Olas. We have talked about flooding here in the City of Miami Beach, but in Fort Lauderdale tidal influences are just as regular there, as well. A business owner that I was talking to just a month ago was expecting to expand his lease into the space next door and grow. After the high tides came in and it flooded his store two inches and he saw what happened to the roadway, he said, ''Well, I am not going to take the lease next door, I am not even going to stay here on Las Olas Boulevard, I am going to move further inland.''

And so it is an interesting conversation because where he moves inland is going—moving inland isn't just the solution because there are 1,800 linear miles of canal systems that drain Broward County.

So understanding where those areas of vulnerability are—that they are not just associated with the coast—when that business makes that decision—and making sure that information is available to the public on our webpage—those things will help people make the kind of decisions that they need that will then make us more resilient and hopefully help our bottom line.

Senator NELSON. And so are you all going to have to spend all kinds of money to help protect Las Olas?

Ms. JACOBS. The City of Fort Lauderdale—I didn't go into this in my notes, but the City of Fort Lauderdale has just come out with their projections, and it is in the hundreds of millions of dollars to address flooding throughout the streets, throughout the City of Fort Lauderdale.

And you have many cities that are dealing with the same issues. And it isn't just those issues, but there are certain cities that don't have their own wastewater utility. And so what are they going to do when the one that they are drawing from, if it is an eastern utility, for example, if they have to go to another new system and that system isn't designed for the capacity to handle all these new users?

So the problem that we are going to be experiencing isn't just about flooding. It is about the loss of freshwater, where you are going to find the money for all of these different systems, and how you are going to prioritize them.

That, I think, is the most important part about what the four counties and all the cities underlying us are working together on, which is to understand where those priorities are, so that when we do want to go after additional dollars, whether it is the State or the Federal side, as we did with the City of Miami Beach, which is to understand who among us is the most vulnerable here and who can we go support.

That is a different idea for local governments to take, because generally it is all for one, you know, and none for the others. So it is a different conversation that we are all leading ourselves into having to take because of circumstances.

Senator NELSON. Dr. Bloetscher, do any other infrastructure projects come to mind for you that would have to be addressed shortly?

Mr. BLOETSCHER. I think the biggest ones that we would need to start looking at, we need to look at canal structures, those structures that we talked about earlier, moving them closer to the coast.

The issue is that if we can pick the ridge and try to put the protection mechanisms along there, there is the potential then for, you know, if you have 80 or 90 percent of the property is actually west of that ridge, you have the opportunity to start installing incrementally the infrastructure to do that.

So that would be one. And, of course, that is not controlled by any local government. It is controlled by the South Florida Water Management District and the Corps of Engineers.

That is kind of this thing where a lot of this stuff will occur locally. Each municipality is addressing the areas where they see flooding in their community and things like that. But there are these regional things that are going to lie outside that, and one of those is dealing with canal structures.

I think there is research that needs to be done on looking at the infiltration concept to see how well we can drain roads. We know we can drain land, but how well can we pinpoint that just to roads.

And I will echo your comment about water supply is a problem. It is already restricted. Going to saltwater really isn't the answer because it drives the power costs up. So can we come up with a scheme where we can take all this excess stormwater—because what I see in the future is, it is not that we don't have enough water, which is kind of the mentality we have been running on for years dealing with water supply. We will have plenty of water. The problem is it is not necessarily going to be in the place or in the timing or of the quality that we want to do for water supply.

So there is some effort that needs to be done there. We have time to do some of that research and investigation, which needs to occur now as opposed to later. Because one of the things that we looked at, as we look at adaptation planning for communities—and we have done a couple of those, and we have done some work here on Miami Beach, as well—we pick milestones. So when we get to six inches, what should we have done? When we get to a foot, what should we have done?

And the benefit of that for local officials is that you are not putting infrastructure out there and then we don't need it for 30 years because, you know, the tide doesn't rise as fast as you thought or vice versa. At the same time, you are not waiting so long that all of a sudden a crisis is upon you and now we have this, ''Oh, we regret that we didn't start this earlier.''

So, from a planning perspective, we need to embellish the toolbox quite a bit. And there is a lot of work that needs to be done before we say that, you know, the solution for Las Olas is X, Y, and Z. We want to make sure those work.

Senator NELSON. Would you or someone else knit together how the addressing of the problems of flooding with the infrastructure projects, how can that be helped knit together with the billions of dollars that we are spending in the restoration of the Everglades and trying to turn the Everglades back closer to what Mother Nature intended, instead of a flood-control project that was started three-quarters of a century ago?

Mr. BLOETSCHER. Yes, the issue there is all about water quality. I mean, the easy thing to do in the western communities is pick the stormwater up and put it across the dike into the Everglades. But you have a huge phosphorus and nitrogen-type problem. So the Corps and the Water Management District have been working on trying to find some, you know, STAs to try to treat that.

I think you are going to see more of that, but there is research that needs to be done, because one of the questions is, where does that water need to go? And we can put a lot of water right across the dike, but the problem is, with the porous limestone, it is going to come right back on you. So you haven't really solved the problem; you are just pumping water in a circle. So how do we get it into the right place?

And let me make a note about the Everglades too. As sea level rises, you know, the low area in Shark Valley of the Everglades is at, like, four feet on I–75, Alligator Alley, and it gets lower as you go. Well, you are going to see saltwater climbing up that, which then potentially threatens wellfields. The southern end of the Everglades will become a very large saltwater swamp at some point. And the only way to really counterbalance that is to figure out a way to get more water into the Everglades to raise the head, which will alter the ecosystem out there fairly significantly.

Inches matter. And when we start adding many more inches of water, however we do that, it will have a fairly significant change. And there are some Federal policies that would need to be evaluated in that. Because the idea is, "Don't change Mother Nature," but——

Senator NELSON. Can you think of—and I will get to some of the other panelists. Can you think of any other communities or areas of the globe that have handled this problem, that are trying to meet a solution to this problem, that we could learn from?

Mr. BLOETSCHER. New Orleans a little bit, but different lessons, perhaps, because that is kind of a low-lying area. In Florida, ultimately, if you use, you know, the railroad corridor as your breakpoint, it is kind of a natural dike that exists there, and you do have all this lower land to the west. So there are some things to learn there.

There absolutely are some things to learn from the Dutch. There absolutely are some things to learn from the Italians in Venice. There are some other areas that are going to have to deal with this, so it will be interesting to see what the folks do in Bangladesh. They have way more people exposed to low-lying land than we do.

So I think there are some good examples out there to learn from. And we have actually been in contact—last fall, we had a discussion with the Dutch. We are involved in a process that the city put on.

Senator NELSON. Dr. Sellers, I would like to expand the scope here and ask you—we have clearly identified the problem. We have looked locally at some of the manifestations of the problem. And we have talked about some of the things that we can do in the short term.

Are mitigation efforts like improving energy efficiency and reducing our reliance on fossil fuels, is that worthwhile? Does that have an effect here?

Mr. SELLERS. I think all the IPCC projections show with pretty good confidence that the climate change we are going to get directly scales to the amount of fossil fuel we burn. It is almost a straight line in terms of temperature increase versus amount of fossil fuel burned.

So it is going to be an intricate and difficult business of trying to reduce our fossil fuel use while maintaining our economies, but, ultimately, it is going to be something that I think we are going to have to manage as a species.

Senator NELSON. Would you describe for the record of our committee the greenhouse effect?

Mr. SELLERS. The greenhouse effect is where you have some gases like carbon dioxide or methane in the atmosphere that allow the sunlight to come through. They are transparent, if you like, to sunlight. But to the heat that is trying to get off the surface, in terms of infrared radiation—that is the heat you can feel from a fire or something—it acts like a blanket. It traps that energy in the atmosphere. And some of that energy gets redirected back to the surface—that extra energy.

And that is the greenhouse effect. It is just like being inside a regular greenhouse.

Senator NELSON. And so the temperature of the Earth rises.

Mr. SELLERS. That is correct. If the energy coming in doesn't match the energy going out and there is an imbalance, the energy has to go somewhere, and it is used to heat up the Earth.

As I said earlier, most of it goes into heating up the oceans, and that is what we have seen over the last century or so. Ninety percent of the energy has gone to heat up the oceans, and about seven percent has been used to melt ice. And that is the interesting business for sea level rise. It is the change in the ice sheets that is going to have, we expect, a big impact on sea level rise over the next century.

Senator NELSON. And most of that CO_2 [carbon dioxide] is in fact as a result of—most of the energy being developed is coming from—fossil fuels.

Mr. SELLERS. Most of it is from fossil-fuel burning. There is a significant contribution from cement production, as well. So it is human activity.

Senator NELSON. I won't ask you the question, what we are going to do to get other countries—particularly China comes to mind. But recently one of our fellow senators was nominated and confirmed to be the present Ambassador to China, and I told him that my present to him, my going-away present to Senator Baucus was going to be a surgical mask for him to wear in Beijing. And that is not a joke, unfortunately.

So maybe it is going to take that for other people to start to realize that other countries have got to get with this.

And, of course, anybody want to comment on these international organizations, like there is one called the IPCC, that is trying to grapple around that?

Dr. Sellers?

Mr. SELLERS. I would just make one comment, that I think the scientific community has taken the stance that it is our job to produce the very best information for everybody. The information is not just what we see, but it is what our models, which are based on very sound physics—it is what our models think is likely to happen.

So we are here to provide the information. Trying to figure out the best way to thread the world's economy through the rapids ahead of us is a job for the public and policymakers.

Ms. JACOBS. And, Senator, if I could, in response to your question, I think it is super-important that the United States of America becomes a real leader. If we want to talk about what other countries ought to be doing, we ought to be talking about what we do here first. Until this country gets serious about funding alternative energy sources——

[Applause.]

Ms. JACOBS. You know, you do what you can. We can't really change what other countries are doing, but we sure can be responsible for our own.

So looking at alternative energy funding, we look at what we are doing within our own policymaking within our cities and counties. And we know that each of us, even in our own homes, can make significant changes.

And I would point to a tiny little statistic, but when you look across the country, what it could change. The amount of fuel that is being used to mow lawns, trim hedges, all of that, you could run a weed whacker or a lawnmower in your yard for one hour and produce the same particulates that you could if you got in your car, drove to Flagstaff, Arizona, and back, from Fort Lauderdale, back again.

So when we talk about all the different ways in which we are contributing, there are a lot of ways in which we can make changes. In Broward County, we set up a system called NatureScape Broward, which takes an example of what you could do in your own yard, school, or business. And the idea was, wherever you might stand in the County, there would be another certified property within a quarter-mile of that place. Today, we have well over 3,000 certified properties that have taken this idea of sustainability and husbandry and attached it to what we are doing individually.

So it starts individually. It really needs to go to the next level, which is broader than just our states, but to the funding that is coming out of the Federal Government.

Senator NELSON. All of you have been spectacular, and the record is pretty complete with what you have testified. There is one thing more that I want to get on the record.

Dr. Sellers, we have been facing budget cuts at NASA, which means that we may not be able to continue to get some of these satellites that provide the data for the measurements that you have shown. As a matter of fact, we have a gap up until 2017.

[A cell phone rings, playing music]

Senator NELSON. That is very good dance music.

We have a gap. Would you explain for the record, please, what the gap is and what some kind of budget cutting that would prohibit future satellites on these measurements would do to our ability to understand what is happening to our planet?

Mr. SELLERS. Well, thanks for the opportunity.

First of all, it is really important to understand that when you are studying something like climate, where you are looking at a lot of natural variability, no two years are alike. You have to keep an eye on the system. You need a continuous set of mutually reinforcing measurements, and you have to keep them going. And this requires a significant investment across a portfolio of satellite instruments, not just one.

So, for example, we were talking earlier about, we have two ways of keeping track of the ice masses on the planet. One is using lasers from space that measure the altitude of ice sticking up off the surface. And the other is a gravity measurement system that is beautifully complicated, but the way it works is it actually weighs the amount of ice sitting on top of Greenland and Antarctica.

So we want to keep these continuous measurements going because you can see it is very important to track rates of change and how much these contribute to sea level rise. So I would say it is vitally important that we sustain investments in the whole portfolio.

Mr. BLOETSCHER. Do you mind if I add——

Senator NELSON. Doctor?

Mr. BLOETSCHER.——one thing to that?

I completely agree, being able to get satellite imagery is really important. It is what we rely on to do a bunch of our work. But I don't think we want to neglect, we have an entire system that USGS and NOAA monitor on the ground what is actually happening—water gauges, groundwater, and things like that. That is equally as important, because what happens is those two things go together.

And I know the budget cut issue has hit USGS, NASA, and all those agencies, but those monitoring programs that have been funded at the Federal level are critical to being able to get a good handle on all of these climate issues, not just in Florida but nationally and around the world.

Mr. SELLERS. I would agree that the combination of satellite and surface measurements is crucial. You can't really get far without both of these.

Senator NELSON. Does our excellent staff have any questions that you would ask?

Well, I want to thank everybody for participating. And I want to thank the panel. You are obviously experts at what you have testified. And for the record, as a Committee of the U.S. Senate, we are most appreciative.

I am going to call this to the attention of several of our Senators that have formed a task force on climate change. And these are some Senators that happen to be members of the Commerce Committee, others are not.

I am also going to call it to the attention of some of my friends in the Senate that believe that there is no data that is showing climate change. And I hope that we can continue to keep this discussion going so that we can come to some reasonable conclusions of what we need to continue to do before it is too late.

Five hundred years ago, Ponce de Leon discovered La Florida. And it was this bountiful land that he called "Florida" because it was Pascua de Flores at the time that he arrived. And then, over the years, we have had the changes that you all have chronicled.

And so I am very, very grateful to you for your testimony.

And the meeting is adjourned.

[Whereupon, at 11:45 a.m., the hearing was adjourned.]

73

This page intentionally left blank.

74

This page intentionally left blank.

75

This page intentionally left blank.